OPEN HEAVENS

Anthonia Adeyeye

OPEN HEAVENS

Copyright © 2020 by **Anthonia Adeyeye**

ISBN: 978-1-944652-99-9

Printed in the United States of America. All rights reserved solely by the publisher. This book or parts thereof may not be reproduced in any form, stored in a retrieval system, or transmitted in any form by any means - electronic, mechanical, photocopy. Unless otherwise noted, Bible quotations are taken from the Holy Bible, New King James Version. Copyright 1982 by Thomas Nelson, Inc., publishers. Used by permission.

Published By:
Cornerstone Publishing
A division of Cornerstone Creativity Group LLC
Info@thecornerstonepublishers.com
www.thecornerstonepublishers.com

Author's Information

For speaking engagement or to order bulk copies of this books please write to:

Dr. Anthonia Adeyeye
Adeyeye Evangelistic Ministries (AEM)
P.O Box 810
West Hempstead, NY 11552
E-mail: dranthonia@alcministries.com
Website: www.alccwinnershouse.org

CONTENTS

Dedication..7
Acknowledgments..9
Preface..13

Part 1: Understanding Open Heavens

1. Facts About Open Heavens..25
2. A Personal Open Heavens Experience.......................35
3. Full View Of Open Heavens......................................47
4. Blessings Of Open Heavens......................................55

Part 2: Beneficiaries of Open Heavens

5. Uplifting Encounters...69
6. Noah: Uncommon Favor From Open Heavens........73
7. Ezekiel: Supernatural Visitations Through Open Heavens...93
8. Blessings From Ezekiel's Open Heavens.................105

9. Ezekiel: Visions of God, Word of God and Hand of God..115

10. Jesus Christ: Divine Seal of Approval From Open Heavens...125

11. Sundry Wonders From Open Heavens....................139

12. Unlocking The Heavens Above You........................149

Prayer Declarations..167

About the Author   171

DEDICATION

To men, women, boys, and girls, who, like me, have gone through or is going through challenges, valleys, and difficulties of life.

God will open His heavens upon you, and the challenges, difficulties, and valley experiences will turn into testimonies, miracles, and celebrations, in Jesus' name.

ACKNOWLEDGMENTS

My unending appreciation goes to God, my Father, my Helper, my Sustainer, my Protector, my Provider, my Forgiver, my beautifier, my lifter, and the God of Open Heavens (the list of who You are to me is endless). Your love for me amazes me, thank You for revealing Yourself to me as my "Daddy." Thank You for always protecting me. Thank You for the supernatural experiences. Thank You for the visions, the revelations, and the testimonies You have been downloading upon me since the writing of this book – Open Heavens. I am forever grateful for Your showers of unending love to me.

To my considerate, diplomatic, straight forward, humble, and very wise husband, my friend, my helper, my coach, my mentor, and teacher, Dr. Festus Adeyeye – my endless gratitude to you! Thanks for being a genuine man of God in secret and in public. Thanks for being a physical, touchable example of God's love and God's long suffering – thanks for being the voice of reason in my life. Your teachings of God's Word continue to help in maturing me, shaping me, and challenging me to climb up higher. I truly celebrate and appreciate the Grace and the anointing of God upon your life, and I love you dearly. Thank you!

My continuous, thunderous, wondrous love and appreciation to all my children. Thanks for your contributions in making this book a reality, I love you all, piece by piece. I am always so thrilled to be around you all, and I cherish the memories of the eleven of you sitting around during family time. I am expecting your number to increase more and more as I expect more sons-in-love and daughters-in-love; make it snappy, guys! Lol! Thanks for loving the Lord, thanks for making "Mothering" peaceful, joyful, and rewarding. You all are so uniquely different, but you all are deeply rooted in my heart. You all mean so much and are so special to me individually and collectively. God bless you all, I love you!

To all the grandchildren – the thoughts of you in my heart gives me unending laughter and indescribable joys. God bless you all.

I thank God for my siblings – The Amazing Grace, the bond of love between us is forever sealed with the Blood of Jesus. You make my life joyful, beautiful, and fun filled. Thank you for being the best and loving siblings anyone would pray to have. I love you all.

To my brothers and sisters all over the world, God bless you!

To my ALCC families, in Winners House and ALCC worldwide, the God of Abundant Life Ministries will open the heavens above you. Your lives will take speed in the right directions, your joys will have no end, and your breakthroughs will be limitless, in Jesus' name.

To my Chief Editor, Blessing Adedolapo Adeyeye, you should have told me your day job as an attorney will make the editing of this book longer than normal – lol! Thanks for offering to edit the book despite your busy schedules. I love you.

God bless Pastor Gbenga Showunmi and his team, you are a blessing to the world!

To the readers of this book, I pray that you will start to experience the same open heavens experiences that I have been experiencing since the writing of this book. God has been opening the heavens above me in the midst of large and small crowds of people – God has been showing me visions, giving me revelations, and amazing testimonies.

Get ready, it's your turn for OPEN HEAVENS!

PREFACE

I am so delighted to welcome you to this glorious exploit we are about to embark upon with this book. It is an exploit that will launch you into an unprecedented realm of life-changing revelations and groundbreaking wonders. Get set for a mighty shift that will touch every aspect of your life.

My prayer for you as you begin to read is contained in these lines from the popular song, *Baba*, by Sonnie Badu:

Open the floodgates in abundance and cause your rain to fall on me

Baba, we're in your presence, let it rain

Oh your rain, let it fall on me

We're in your presence, let it rain

Oh your rain, let it fall on me

I pray that God will open His floodgates of abundance and lavish His treasures upon you. I pray that His heavenly rain will remove every stagnancy, dryness, and drought in your life. Above all, I pray that by the time you are done reading this book, you would have been spiritually empowered, uncommonly anointed, and divinely equipped to draw closer to God and pray prayers to open the heavens.

But then, you may wonder, why exactly do I have to read this book? There are indeed several reasons why the Holy Spirit has caused this book to be written and made available to you at this time. To begin with, this is a God-inspired book. One great evening, as I prepared to have one of my telephone prayer conferences, the Holy Spirit gave me different revelations on the subject of open heavens. He explained the subject using various examples of people who enjoyed God's open heavens and individuals who had difficulties in life due to the fact that the heavens closed upon them. At that same moment, God spoke to my spirit that some of the leaders I was to pray with only needed the heavens above them to open up. He said that once the heavens opened up over their lives, they would begin to experience dimensions of success beyond the labors of their hands. He added that they would also begin to enjoy accelerated success beyond their plans and efforts.

As you read this book, this same grace will fall upon you. As you make the declarations in it, you will experience dimensions of success more than the labor of your hands. Accelerated success will be your daily experience, in the name of Jesus.

This book is bound to cause your eyes of understanding to open further. You will begin to see things you ordinarily would not have seen with your natural eyes. This will automatically position your destiny for greater dimensions of blessings. Indeed, open heavens will become your daily experience with the deeper insights that you will gain from this book.

Again, you will find this book of tremendous benefit if you or someone you know are feeling left out of God's blessings or feeling "stuck in the rut." As a Christian, there are times you may feel as if blessings are passing you by and flowing into other people's lives, while you are stagnant or "stuck in the rut." You may feel like blessings are flowing all around you and above you, but not to you. Not that you are unhappy that others are being blessed; you just would like to partake of the blessings of God too. You want to start experiencing your full inheritance already procured with the blood of Jesus.

Nobody likes to be left out of good things, so it is right to have what I call "holy questions," "holy concerns," and "holy self-talks." There is a grace in and on this book which ensures that anyone who reads it will not be left out of God's blessings. God's blessings will not just be flowing to others all around you, but these undeniable blessings will be enjoyed by you and everyone connected to you, in Jesus' name.

I also urge you to read this book if you have what I call a

"holy dissatisfaction" with the current state of your life. There are times that, as a Christian, you know you have climbed or have started climbing the ladder of success, but you are not completely pleased with the pace or level of progress you have attained so far. You might have done all you know to do and all you are taught to do, but you are not experiencing significant success. You know that there is more to life than the current place you are standing. You may have often quoted Proverbs 4:18, "But the path of the just is like the shining sun, that shines ever brighter unto the perfect day." You may have seen the first "brighter," but are yet to experience the "ever brighter" dimension of success. If this is you, then you need to read this book.

I guarantee that as you pray the prayers in this book, the heavens will open over your life, career, ministry, and whatever you lay your hands upon. Things will get better and better, and your life will shine brighter and brighter, in Jesus' name. This is your own "now" season, and it is your turn to experience the blessings of open heavens.

You should also read this book if you have family members or you know Christians who are in one or more of the conditions that I have just mentioned. The grace of God will empower you to help change their lives.

You will also find this book a great source of blessing as an entrepreneur who wants to have extraordinary business success. To run a successful business or be a trailblazer in your chosen career path, you need the heavens to open upon your destiny and upon whatever you lay your hands on. The blessings coming from your open heavens plus the labor of your hands will take you to dimensions of success that cannot be contested.

Moreover, as a growing believer, this book will teach you how to use Bible verses to pray. Most of the prayers in this book are extracted from the scriptures preceding them. By the time you get to the third chapter, you would have gained an in-depth understanding of how to pray scripturally. If you already know how to do this, the grace will increase and abound more and more upon you.

I am personally persuaded that even if you are reading this book as a prayer warrior, the grace of praying will abound and increase in your life. On the other hand, if prayer has been an uphill task for you, the anointing in this book will shatter the forces contending with your prayer life. Thereafter, scriptural prayers will become a lifestyle for you, and you will begin to find praying a great delight.

There are many benefits in praying scripturally, as we will be doing in this book. God Himself said we should command Him concerning His work, and if we pray according to His will, He will hear us and answer us. He says in Isaiah 45:11 and John 15:14, "Thus says the Lord, the Holy One of Israel, and his Maker: Ask Me of things to come concerning My sons; And concerning the work of My hands, you command Me…Now this is the confidence that we have in Him, that if we ask anything according to His will, He hears us."

This book will also thoroughly enrich your life if you are a pastor, an apostle, a teacher, minister, leader, prayer warrior, or any other laborer in God's vineyard. You should be interested in praying for other people and the body of Christ as a whole, so that there can be breakthroughs and advancement in God's kingdom.

Overall, I assure you that, as you read this book, your "faucet drippings of blessings" will turn to "full blast faucet overflow of blessings." There was a time the Holy Spirit gave me an analogy on this. When you open your water faucet and it is dripping drop by drop, it takes a longer time for your bucket to be full. However, if the same faucet is opened to full blast capacity, your bucket can be filled with water within minutes. Some Christians experience the blessings of God in faucet drippings – that is, in little drops - while others enjoy the full blast faucet overflow of blessings. In case you feel you are in the "faucet drippings" group or even any other group at all, get ready for a dramatic and sudden shifting of your destiny.

Let me congratulate you again, for you have come to a new season in your life – the season of undeniable blessings. You have read about others being blessed beyond measure. You have seen with your own eyes uncountable blessings of God in other peoples' lives. You have heard amazing stories and testimonies of others, but now it is your turn to experience an overflow of God's blessings through His OPEN HEAVENS. As you read this book, your permanent living experience will be as contained in Deuteronomy 28:12: "The LORD will open for you His good treasure house, the heavens, to give rain to your land in its season and to bless all the work of your hand; and you will lend to many nations, but you will not borrow."

Once again, I pray for you that showers of breakthroughs, miracles, signs, and wonders will be released upon you, as you read this book. Undisputable proofs and manifestations of success will be seen in your life. As you wholeheartedly receive the revelations given by the Holy Spirit in this book and pray the inspired prayers, your own heavens will open and grace to pray and intercede will be abundantly released upon you to do exploits, in Jesus' name.

How To Use The Book

This is primarily meant to be a prayer book and you will find the expositions in each chapter interspersed with powerful prayer points. This is done to keep you within the spectrum of the move of the Holy Spirit. The point is for you to go beyond having theoretical knowledge to getting practical and tangible manifestations in every area of your life.

You will find different kinds of prayer here. Some are written as personal prayers points and some are prayer declarations. The personal prayer points are prayers that you can use daily, over and over, when praying for yourself and your loved ones. The prayer declarations are prophetic declarations pronounced on you by the author. Ensure to say an "amen" to each of these declarations in affirmation of your assurance that it will come to pass as decreed. You can also personalize these prayers and use them daily. They can also be used as prophetic prayers for your loved ones.

While writing this book, the Holy Spirit quickened my spirit that while readers should pray the prayer points in it, every reader should also get ready have the mantle and spontaneity of prayer fall upon them. What this means is that, as you pray the prayers in this book, you will understand how to pray scripturally and the mantle of prayer will also drop upon your life. There will be no dreading of prayer and no praying amiss. You will master the art of praying, and you will become a Holy Ghost empowered prayer-generating machine.

Prayer Declarations

In Jeremiah 7:24, God said concerning the people of Judah that they went backward instead of forward. Their fathers had also gone through a similar experience – a journey that should have taken just 11 days took them 40 years. I decree and declare over your life that you will not go backward. You will not regress. You will not be stagnant. You will not go round in circles over the same issues. I speak over your life – backward never, forward ever. Forward ever in your destiny; forward ever in your career; forward ever in the works of your hands, in Jesus' name. The issues of your life will not be prolonged. I rebuke the spirit of delay, stagnancy, going round in circles, and late achievement in your life, in Jesus' name. **Let's proceed to open the heavens in full blast!**

PART 1
UNDERSTANDING OPEN HEAVENS

1
FACTS ABOUT OPEN HEAVENS

As we will be discussing later, there are some crucial facts you must know about open heavens that will help you to have a clear picture of what an open heaven means. Knowing these facts will help you to have a better understanding about life experiences and how to enforce the blessings that should accompany you and your loved ones. Here are the facts:

1. The heavens can be opened over a person, groups of people, a nation, or nations. The fact that the heavens can be opened is seen in many scripture passages. Here is one of them in Deuteronomy 28:12: "The LORD will open for you His good treasure house, the heavens, to give rain to your land in its season and to bless all the work of your hand; and you will lend to many nations, but you will not borrow."

2. We find it clearly stated here that the heavens can be

opened. We find that these open heavens can refer to God's treasure house, and God is very much willing to open this treasure house for us.

3. There are manifold blessings to be enjoyed when the heavens are opened upon a life. This fact can also be seen in Deuteronomy 28:12, as well as in many other verses of the bible. This book is actually about the blessings derived through open heavens. These blessings are numerous, and they have been used as prayer points and written on the pages of this book. As you pray these blessings over your life, you will begin to see manifestations of God's glory in every area of your life.

4. As the heavens can be opened, so also can they be closed upon a life, business, family, city, or nation. This fact can be seen in Deuteronomy 28:23-24, "The heaven which is over your head shall be bronze [giving no rain and blocking all prayers], and the earth which is under you, iron [hard to plow and yielding no produce]. The LORD will make the rain of your land powder and dust; from heaven it will come down on you until you are destroyed." This shows that when the heavens are closed, blessings are prevented from flowing down. When the heavens close upon a life, the earth also becomes hard and unyielding. Rain becoming dust symbolizes lack of productivity and progress in a life under closed heavens.

Pray this:

In the name of Jesus, I will not experience the destructions and devastations of a closed heaven. My heavens will not be closed; they will remain opened and God's blessings will flow into my life. The work of my hands is blessed and everything I lay my hands upon will prosper. I will cooperate with God and will make decisions that will foster continuous opening of my heavens, in Jesus' name (Deuteronomy 28: 12, 23-24).

When the heavens are closed upon a life, curses that bring destructions, droughts, and devastations are suffered by the individual. Let me tell you about a dear lady, I'll call her "Sister Frustration" because of the depth of anguish that she had been through. This sister had been so frustrated with her life that she had attempted killing herself on four different occasions. One time, she told me she had been led by God to discuss her situation with me. Yes, it may surprise you that Sister Frustration is a Christian. This dear lady had lived in at least four continents. She had moved from one country to the other and changed addresses several times, but she had never succeeded. Her life had been filled with frustrations upon frustrations.

Sister Frustration had lived under hardship, hatred, and difficulty in every country and cities she lived in. Any little blessing she had experienced came after uncountable years of failure. Every area of her life had been a drag. Getting married was a tough and protracted battle.

Eventually when she got married, the man was struggling with homosexuality. It always took sister Frustration longer years to obtain a little blessing that would take other people a few days.

I eventually set up an appointment to meet with Sister Frustration. She had to drive from another state to meet with me in New York. And guess what? She had three accidents between her destination and New York! On my end, despite the fact that I knew of the appointment, many emergencies came up that almost made the appointment impossible. The devil threw every trick in order for the appointment not to hold.

When I eventually met this beautiful lady, I felt bad for her because of the many disasters she had been through in life. Through prayers, I saw a thick impenetrable cloud of heaviness all around her. The cloud moved all around her and covered her like a blanket! Nothing good was being released upon her from above and the cloud also blocked blessings from below. Thank God for Jesus, who ended years of demonic darkness and wickedness in her life. To God be the glory, Sister Frustration soon became Sister Felicitation. Her former life however was a classic pointer to the fact that when heavens are closed, earth will be hard and unyielding, people will generally be uncooperative, and doors of opportunities will take numerous years to open.

The heavens can open or close on people individually,

or collectively as a family, city or nation. There are many examples of this fact in the Bible and in the lives of people in different parts of the world. One of the biblical examples is the case of Ezekiel. While among a group of people, he experienced open heavens, which others had no clue of. Here is his testimony in Ezekiel 1:1, "Now it came to pass in the thirtieth year, in the fourth month, on the fifth day of the month, as I was among the captives by the River Chebar, that the heavens were opened and I saw visions of God."

Ezekiel was among other people, but he was the only one who experienced open heavens. We will dwell more on this experience of his later on.

Pray this:

Father, in the name of Jesus, after the order of Ezekiel, no matter where I go today, no matter how many people will be where I am, let the heavens above me be opened. The Scripture affirms that God daily loads us with benefits. Therefore, I declare that I will enjoy the blessings and benefits released for this day, in Jesus' name. My family, business, career, and whatever else I do will be singled out for favor, in Jesus' name. All who are connected to me will be selected among the crowd for blessings, in Jesus' name (Ezekiel 1:1; Psalms 68:19).

NEW TESTAMENT BELIEVERS AND OPEN HEAVENS

Before closing this chapter, it is important that I address the belief of some believers that all Christians have open heavens above them because they are New Testament believers. This is not scripturally correct. There is a difference between having an open door to the throne of God and having God open His good treasures, the heavens, upon a life. The former is the redemption right of all believers to access the throne of God for mercy; the latter is open heavens. One is an open door to God, the other is open heavens from God. The former can be enjoyed by Christians at any time, the latter is the prerogative of God, based on His sovereignty. A closed heaven can also come as a result of manipulations and activities of Satan through his spiritual agents – demons, principalities, and powers, as well as his earthly agents.

Let me explain further. All New Testament believers definitely have "an open door" – unblocked and unhindered access to the presence of God, because of the atonement work of our Lord and Savior, Jesus Christ. The veil blocking all men from the presence of God in the temple was rented from top to bottom when Jesus paid for the sins of the world. Matthew 27:50-51 narrates: "And Jesus cried out again with a loud voice, and yielded up His spirit. Then, behold, the veil of the temple was torn in two from top to bottom; and the earth quaked, and the rocks were split."

Consequently, all New Testament believers are enjoined to come to God's presence with boldness. Hebrews 4:14-16 says, "Seeing then that we have a great High Priest who has passed through the heavens, Jesus the Son of God, let us hold fast *our* confession. For we do not have a High Priest who cannot sympathize with our weaknesses, but was in all *points* tempted as *we are, yet* without sin. Let us therefore come boldly to the throne of grace, that we may obtain mercy and find grace to help in time of need."

This is God's invitation to all New Testament believers. Jesus, as our High Priest, is interceding on our behalf before the Father. All believers can approach the throne of God to obtain mercy. Since God is such a generous Father, believers will not just find mercy, they will also find grace to accompany them to help them in life.

All the early disciples had this invitation, so also do today's Christians. But despite the invitation to God's presence, God still chose to open His heavens upon Peter, as recorded in Acts 10:9-10, "The next day, as they went on their journey and drew near the city, Peter went up on the housetop to pray, about the sixth hour. Then he became very hungry and wanted to eat; but while they made ready, he fell into a trance and **saw heaven opened** and an object like a great sheet bound at the four corners, descending to him and let down to the earth."

This **open heaven** experience by Peter is clearly different from the general **open door** the believers of then and now have to the presence of God.

Another good example was the experience of Paul (formerly Saul) on his way to Damascus: "As he journeyed, he came near Damascus, and **suddenly a light shone around him from heaven**. Then he fell to the ground, and heard a voice saying to him, "Saul, Saul, why are you persecuting Me?" And he said, "Who are You, Lord?"

Then the Lord said, "I am Jesus, whom you are persecuting. It *is* hard for you to kick against the goads" (Acts 9:3-5).

Saul, in the above scriptures was not even a New Testament believer yet, but God chose to give him a supernatural encounter through having the heavens above him opened up.

In His sovereignty, God can make it His prerogative, at any point, to intercept in a person's life by having His heavens open upon such an individual. So there is a clear difference between the general invitation of God to all believers and God's choice to open His heavens upon a life. Neither of the events can be discounted. Jesus paid with His life to give us access to God's presence and that same God of mercy and grace will favor you with open heavens experiences, in Jesus' name. In fact, the open door which is your access to God's presence, is the easiest way for you to ask God to open His heavens upon you for special favors.

Pray this:

- In the name of Jesus, the open access I have into God's presence will not be wasted. I received the grace to enjoy and maximize my relationship with God. He will open His heavens over me and be the Dew to my life. My life will blossom like the lily, and God will showcase and demarcate my destiny with His glory, in Jesus' name (Hebrews 4:16; Hosea 14:5)

- I pray that after the likeness of Ezekiel, wherever I go today, whether I am in the midst of others, my family, or on the job with my colleagues, heavens will open over me. Blessings of God will flow into all areas of my life. My mouth will be filled with laughter and my tongue shall sing glorious songs of the Lord. All eyes shall see that the Lord has done great and might things for me, in Jesus' name (Ezekiel 1: 1; Psalms 126: 2-3)

- As God in His mercy supernaturally opened His heavens upon Saul and subsequently corrected his past errors and commissioned him for a unique assignment, on this day, I declare that my heavens are opened. God's hands are upon my destiny and grace for error correction is released upon me. All errors of my past are cancelled and erased. In the name of Jesus, as Saul changed to Paul, anointing to cause changes for the fulfillment of my destiny is at work in my life now, in Jesus' name. I also pray that as Paul was elevated by grace above others, God will elevate me, my career, my business, my family, and everything and everyone connected to me, in Jesus' name (Acts 9:3, 13:9; 1 Corinthians 15:10).

Prayer Declarations

The satanic angel, Prince of Persia, tried to block the heavens above Daniel by delaying the answers to his prayers (Daniel 10:13). I take authority and dominion over any satanic agenda in your life. Every manipulation of darkness through evil angels and satanic day and night operators over your life is destroyed, in the name of Jesus. Whatever valuable thing that has been lost in your life will be found. Whatever has been vandalized in your destiny will be restored. God will force out your riches and blessings out of the mouth and bellies of the wicked. God will make you a blessing, and showers of blessings shall fall upon you. The ground beneath your feet will yield its treasures to you, in Jesus' name (Job 20:15; Ezekiel 34: 24-27).

2
A PERSONAL OPEN HEAVENS EXPERIENCE

> "We have escaped like a bird from the snare of the fowlers;
> The trap is broken and we have escaped.
> Our help is in the name of the LORD,
> Who made heaven and earth.
>
> (Psalms 124: 7-8)

Any Christian who has ever been in the valleys of life and has faced many spiritual battles like I have been through can understand and appreciate Psalms 124 in its entirety. If not for the Lord who was fighting on behalf of the Israelites and supporting them, they would have been swallowed up by men and engulfed by the waters of life.

I always read this Psalms using my name to replace Israel's.

This is because I can identify and relate with the message and the experiences they must have gone through. Beloved reader, if not for the Lord who has been my Help and Helper, I would have been dead from many death traps set against my life. God has been my deliverer. He has always risen to the occasion and proven Himself stronger than all the gang-ups of wicked men against my life. God has broken the net of the hunter, and like a bird, I have escaped from the many nets of wickedness set against my life.

By the grace of God, I have been privileged to have many supernatural experiences, including those relating to open heavens. I would like to share my personal experience of open heavens with you, before delving properly into the subject.

The occurrence I am about to share with you is scary but real, and it always generates extra praises from me to God whenever I am praying. I am aware that people are sometimes skeptical, especially about supernatural experiences and occurrences. I understand how the human nature may tend to fight off, resist, argue, or even disbelieve what we sometimes don't understand. Yet, none of these reactions can erase or remove the reality of these supernatural experiences. This was the situation with the man born blind whose eyes Jesus opened. The miracle generated controversies; some people believed, while others doubted. The Jews insisted that Jesus was a sinner, separated from God. The blind man however said something very paramount in John 9:25, "I do not know whether He is a sinner [separated from God]; but one thing I do know, that though I was blind, now I see."

I emphasized the second part of the man's statement because what the man was insinuating was that he couldn't understand the reason they were arguing over his healing – especially as neither their argument nor unbelief could change the fact that he used to be blind, but Jesus had given him sight! Simply put, no one could take his experience away from him, just as I know that none can take mine from me either.

Having provided the above background, travel with me as I share my personal experience of God's mercy and open heavens in my life.

Satanic Package

On Saturday, December 6th, 2014, I almost died without any prior sickness or accident. It was a death planned and orchestrated by Satan and some of his wicked human agents.

Interestingly, two years before then, sometime in 2012, the Holy Spirit had spoken to me and given me a prayer point to be praying daily for my life. I have never heard or read of anybody else who prayed this prayer. The Holy Spirit said to me, "Daughter, I want you to start praying that any evil package, hanging in the atmosphere, waiting for a "time of life" to land upon you, will not land."

As of the time the Holy Spirit gave me this prayer point, I really didn't have the full understanding of the prayer. Still, I obeyed God's instruction and prayed faithfully that the evil package would not land upon my life. So it was on this fateful day, Saturday, December 6, 2014, that an evil package was released. I give God all the glory that, in His mercy, He did not allow the enemy to prevail over my life.

It happened that that particular Saturday had been slated for workers' training in our church, Abundant Life Christian Ministries. The training went very well; in fact, I was privileged to be one of the speakers. I was in very good spirits after the meeting. There was a senior citizen in the ministry that I wanted to buy clothes for, so that she could have good and warm clothes in readiness for the cold season. My husband went with me to the store to shop for clothes for this older lady. Suddenly, as soon as we paid the cashier, I felt like somebody was sucking the air out of my body. I couldn't breathe! I was panting and gasping for air. It was very scary, because I had never had asthma and was never sickly. The only times I had slept over in a hospital were for baby deliveries; God has favored me with divine health and to Him be all the glory.

My condition began to worsen and I had to open my mouth wide in order to force air into my lungs. My husband rushed me to NYU Winthrop University Hospital. As I walked briskly to the emergency room, I kept praying and speaking in tongues. I kept affirming the Word of God –

that I would live and not die. I declared that I would not be carried out of the hospital but would walk with my own feet.

At the triage, the form I should have completed was taken away from me as I was in no condition to fill any form. Thank God that the lady attending to me was a Christian. She started praying in tongues also and kept saying "amen" to my prayers. My blood pressure was 179/96. This was a very shocking piece of news as I had always had a normal pressure and was never sickly.

All kinds of tests were done on me, and everything came back negative. I called my four other siblings and alerted them to start praying. My husband, too, was praying tirelessly over me. The doctor attending to me was concerned, as my case was getting worse and nothing seemed to be medically wrong with me, and all tests came back negative.

At a point, I just couldn't pray in English anymore, I kept praying in tongues. Things got worse. I felt my spirit leaving my body; it was moving from my legs to exit my body through my mouth. I knew then that I was dying and that once my spirit left, it was over! As I was praying, the devil was also bombarding my mind with thoughts that he would kill me that night. He said things like, "Give your husband final instructions"; "tell your sisters whatever they need to do after you are gone"!

TIMELY VICTORY

As these evil thoughts were flooding my mind, I was rejecting and canceling them. I began to hear the Holy Spirit praying though my mouth fresh prayers points, "Lord, make good your word and promises over my life. You promise that I will preach your word, and all other promises spoken over my life are yet to take place. Intervene, O Lord."

As I laid on that hospital bed, breathing through my mouth, I never stopped the prayers. At a point, a very cool wind blew over me from my feet to my head. Instantly, I knew this was the wind from the presence of God. I said underneath my breath, "Lord, I thank you for this cool wind from your presence." I knew immediately that I was healed. I knew the wind was the supernatural presence of God; it was soothing and refreshing on my body. My husband said he heard me when I said, "LORD, THANK YOU FOR THE COOL WIND FROM YOUR PRESENCE."

My beloved, as soon as this wind of God blew over me, EVERYTHING went back to NORMAL! Praise the awesome, merciful, gracious, faithful, kind, and powerful God that we serve. All my vitals went back to normal without any medication! The doctor was surprised and she expressed it, saying, "This is very strange."

Divine Explanation

I was soon discharged from the hospital but could not sleep due to the horrific, near-death experience. I spent time thanking God, but I told Him I was not going to sleep until He would explain to me the reason I almost died mysteriously. I was bothered that the enemy almost took my life and I was supposed to be God's daughter, a Christian, a Pastor's wife, and a Pastor!

The Holy Spirit asked me to sit up and get a pen. Then He began to give me understanding. I will not be able to discuss the root of the "evil package" in this book, but I must emphasize it again that it took God's intervention to cancel the evil agenda slated on the calendar of Satan for me.

I thank God for His mercy. I thank God for a wonderful, prayerful husband, who proved to be a shield and not a door for the enemy to kill me. And I thank God for my wonderful siblings. Praise God!

Open Heavens Angle

So, why am I calling this experience my open heavens experience? One of the definitions of open heavens, as you will read in the next chapter, is: "The supernatural visitation and intervention from God in which God uses any of His supernatural ammunitions to cause changes in a natural situation or condition."

God used His supernatural ammunition of "wind" to blow upon me and the storm ceased instantly. This is similar to what happened in Genesis 8:1, where God caused the wind to blow and the waters receded. It was a supernatural move from heaven that made this to happen.

I believe that God opened the heavens above me on December 6th, 2014. He blew His cool wind over me. He returned my spirit that was already leaving my body back into its place. God supernaturally intervened and destroyed the evil package hanging in the atmosphere, and He demonstrated that His power supersedes the wicked powers of darkness. As the rod of Aaron swallowed the rods of the evil magicians, the power of my God swallowed all the incantations and evil arrangements of Satan over my life. He broke the back of wickedness and completely destroyed every plan of premature death, concussions, and evil formulas. Exodus 7:12 says, "For every man threw down his staff and they turned into serpents, but Aaron's staff swallowed up their staffs."

Pray this:

- Father, in the name of Jesus, after the order of showdown between Aaron and the magicians, give a showdown to every enemy of my soul. As the rod of Aaron swallowed the evil rods, let every enemy refusing to repent be swallowed by their own evil plans, in Jesus' name. The Bible says in Proverbs 26;27, "Whoever digs a pit [for another man's feet] will fall into it, And he who rolls a stone [up a hill to do mischief], it will come back on him." I declare that whoever is trying to injure me will injure themselves. Father, I pray in the name of Jesus, intervene in my life. Every stronghold of darkness in my family, break right now, in Jesus' name. The power of God swallows up all agendas of darkness over my life, in Jesus name.

- It is written in Psalms 124:1-8, "If it had not been the Lord who was on our side, Let Israel now say— If it had not been the Lord who was on our side, When men rose up against us, Then they would have swallowed us alive, When their wrath was kindled against us; Then the waters would have overwhelmed us, The stream would have gone over our soul; Then the swollen waters Would have gone over our soul. Blessed be the Lord, Who has not given us as prey to their teeth. Our soul has escaped as a bird from the snare of the fowlers; The snare is broken, and we have escaped. Our help is in the name of the Lord, Who made heaven and earth."

Pray this:

- I decree that God is on my side; whoever rises against me will fall for my sake.

- Whoever sets any trap for me will fall into it; he who digs a pit falls into it. All my haters will fall into their own pits, in Jesus' name.

- This day, is my day of release, I have escaped all evil arrangements, evil pronouncements, and all evil expectations, in Jesus' name.

- Whatever has been holding me down, break your hold over me, in Jesus' name.

- The Bible says that strangers must come out of hiding and fade away (Psalms 18:45). I command anything poisonous, injurious, or satanic that I may have swallowed to come out and fade away, in Jesus' name.

- I escape the sicknesses of my father's family, in the name of the Lord.

- I decree in Jesus' name that I have escaped sicknesses from my mother's family.

- I escape evil words, pronouncements, and expectations against my life, in Jesus' name.

- I declare that God is my Help and Helper and He is helping me right now, in Jesus' name.

Prayer Declarations

God is the same yesterday, today, and forevermore. Therefore, I decree in Jesus' name, that the Mighty God, who broke the hold of Satan and stopped premature death in my life, will miraculously intervene in your life right now, in Jesus' name. I pray that God will open His heavens over you now. All negative patterns in your family are nullified. You will not partake of any evil. What stagnates others will lift you. What causes delays in the lives of others will advance your life, in Jesus' name.

God used large hailstones to kill the enemies of Israel. He caused panic in the camp of Arameans by making them to hear sound of chariots, horses, and a great army. I decree, there shall be heavy commotion in the lives of those plotting evil against you, in Jesus' name. All liars and those trying to injure you will be heavily assaulted and defeated, in Jesus' name.

I also decree and declare, if there is any evil package, pattern, pronouncement or expectation hanging in the air, looking or working to land upon you, let the fire of God burn it to ashes, in Jesus' name (Joshua 10:11; 2 Kings 7:6).

3
FULL VIEW OF OPEN HEAVENS

I believe that with all we have explored so far, including the personal testimony I shared in the previous chapter, you should have begun to have a clear picture of the meaning and ramifications of open heavens. Here, however, we will plunge deeper in examining this blessed reality, with particular attention to scriptural perspectives.

Of course, the Bible does not have to explicitly mention that the heavens are opened for a believer to know and accept that God has open heavens. Open heavens occur anytime God interferes in the order of nature, suspending all other arrangements momentarily, until He achieves His goal on earth. Similarly, a believer should know that heavens are opened by God whenever He superimposes spiritual laws on natural processes and scientific laws – indeed, rendering all laws of no effect, or suspending them until He does His will in that period of time.

A classic example of such divine superimposition is found in Joshua 10:12-13: "On the day the LORD gave the Amorites over to Israel, Joshua said to the LORD in the presence of Israel: 'Sun, stand still over Gibeon, and you, moon, over the Valley of Aijalon.' So the sun stood still, and the moon stopped, till the nation avenged itself on its enemies, as it is written in the Book of Jashar. The sun stopped in the middle of the sky and delayed going down about a full day."

We see here that God momentarily superimposed His plan and the prayer of Joshua over both the natural order He had put in place and the scientific theories of man.

OTHER SCRIPTURAL ALLUSIONS

Similar scriptural references which allude to open heavens include:

- Deuteronomy 28:12: "The LORD will open for you His good treasure house, the heavens, to give rain to your land in its season and to bless all the work of your hand; and you will lend to many nations, but you will not borrow."

- Isaiah 64:1,3: "Oh, that You would rend the heavens! That You would come down! That the mountains might shake at Your presence— When You did awesome things *for which* we did not look, You came down, The mountains shook at Your presence."

- Luke 3:21: "When all the people were baptized, it came to pass that Jesus also was baptized; and while He prayed, the heaven was opened."

- Revelation 19:11: "Now I saw heaven opened, and behold, a white horse. And He who sat on him *was* called Faithful and True, and in righteousness He judges and makes war."

From these and other scriptural references, as well as specific revelations from the Holy Spirit to this writer, we can view an open heavens experience as:

- When God literally manifests Himself to a person, family, group, community, or nation, through supernatural experience or experiences.

- When God manifests Himself by giving instructions, directions, affirmation, and confirmation about His plans to a person or group of persons.

- The supernatural visitation of God that rearranges natural orders and laws of earth, that He Himself established, in order to carry out His will on earth.

- The special visitation of God that makes a person enjoy inexplicable and undeniable joy and wellness.

- The supernatural visitation of God upon a recipient or recipients that distinguishes and demarcates them for favor and abundance.

- A supernatural encounter that causes the recipient to enjoy specific benefits that others around them are not experiencing nor enjoying. When the heavens are opened, recipients can see, hear, or receive supernatural things and instructions that others around them are not privy to.

- The supernatural visitation and intervention from God in which He uses any of His supernatural ammunitions to cause changes in a natural situation or condition.

Pray this:

- Father, in the name of Jesus, as I read this book, heavens will open upon my destiny. I will enjoy every blessing that comes through the heavens opening upon a life. I will have supernatural encounters with God. In the name of Jesus, I will receive instructions that will lead to my affirmation, confirmation, and glorification. Heavens will smile upon me. I will be favored by God and man. I will enjoy undeniable joy and wellness, in Jesus' name.

- As I step out today, I decree and declare that God will suspend natural laws, scientific laws, and all laws set by men, for my benefit. None of these laws will stop me or hinder my progress, in Jesus' name.

- God's perfect plans will come to pass speedily in my life. I will be lifted above all hindrances. God will cause me to fly in the high places of life and I will suck honey from rocks, in Jesus' name (Deuteronomy 32:13).

- Note also that you can personalize and create prayer points from some of the definitions of open heavens written above. You can say, for example:

- In the name of Jesus, as I step out today, I decree and declare that God's spiritual laws will override and suspend any natural law, scientific law, or any other law that may want to hinder His plans for my life.

- This day, my life and destiny will experience open heavens and because of this, I will fly in the high places of life and will suck honey in the hard and low places of life, in Jesus' name.

- Father, as I step out today, let your heavens open upon my life and the lives of my loved ones. Help me to hear instructions from you that will cause me to enjoy extra special blessings that others may not see nor even experience.

- Father, in the name of Jesus, as I go to…(Mention wherever you are going today and whatever you are going to do), my life and destiny will not suffer shame; rather, my destiny will experience coloration, beautification, affirmation, confirmation, and glorification, in Jesus' name.

- You can also declare the above prayers daily over your

business, ministry, education, trips [on the road, on the train, in the air etc.], and over anyone and anything that concerns you.

DIMENSIONS OF OPEN HEAVENS

Different recipients of open heavens experienced God's treasures in diverse ways. God is a God of patterns and principles, and He Himself has declared that He does not change. He said in Malachi 3: 6a, "For I *am* the LORD, I do not change." This means that we can learn a lot from the experiences of past recipients of open heavens.

From the testimonies of those who have had encounters with God through open heavens, we see the following dimensions of manifestation:

- Recipients can dream dreams, in which they can literally see heavens opening up for them.

- Recipients of open heavens can see visions. A vision can come when a person is either partly awake or not sleeping at all. Such a person sees images or events and can also hear voices in a flash.

- Recipients of open heavens may see different objects or creatures in their dreams and visions, depending on the objectives of God in their lives. Recipients may see doors, windows, lights, pictures, or angelic beings.

- Recipients of open heavens may tangibly feel divine

presence. Although we walk by faith and not by sight (2 Corinthians 5:7), there are times in which a person can specially feel or sense the presence of God. For instance, the disciples clearly saw Jesus ascend to heaven in Luke 24: 50-52, "And He led them out as far as Bethany, and He lifted up His hands and blessed them. Now it came to pass, while He blessed them, that He was parted from them and carried up into heaven. And they worshiped Him, and returned to Jerusalem with great joy."

Prayer Declarations

I pray for you, reader, that all the blessings that come with open heavens will be your portion throughout this season. As Jesus' disciples returned to Jerusalem in Luke 24: 52 with joy, so also will you return daily to your house with great joy. Great joy will be your daily experiences in all areas of your life. As you embark on your day-to-day activities, you will start and end with great joy daily, in Jesus' name. In line with returning back to your destinations, I pray, Isaiah 51:11 over your life;

Isaiah 51:11 says, "So the redeemed of the LORD will return and come with joyful shouting to Zion; Everlasting joy will be on their heads. They will obtain gladness and joy, and sorrow and sighing will flee away." I declare that wherever you go this day, week, month or year, you will return to your destinations safely. You will always return to Zion – the place of your worship and you will do so with testimonies. You will not be part of those who will travel and not return. I decree that whatever will cause you sorrow or sighing will not come near you. Your portion is gladness and joy daily, in Jesus' name.

4

BLESSINGS OF OPEN HEAVENS

Deuteronomy 28: 1-14 contains many blessings of God that can be enjoyed by believers who walk in obedience to God. One of these blessings is that the heavens will be opened upon us. And when the heavens are opened, there are great and manifold blessings to be enjoyed.

Let's see some of the blessings of open heavens, especially as revealed in Deuteronomy 28:12. After that, we will consider some other blessings of this glorious experience. Deuteronomy 28:12 says, "The LORD will open for you His good treasure house, the heavens, to give rain to your land in its season and to bless all the work of your hand; and you will lend to many nations, but you will not borrow."

It says here that once the heavens are opened upon you, you are guaranteed the following blessings:

1. You will become a "showcase of God's good treasures."

This is what is implied by "**The LORD** will open for you His good treasure house, the heavens…" Dear reader, if a rich family member of yours promises to give you "gifts," maybe for your birthday, you will already be excited over the mention of "gifts." Should this rich individual go a step further to qualify the gift as "good," you will be confident that it will be a big gift. Now, can you now imagine God, who says "The silver is mine and the gold is mine" (Haggai 2:8) and that to Him belong "the cattle on a thousand hills" (Psalms 50:10). This is the same God who is so rich that the whole earth we live in is just His footstool promising to open for you **His good treasure** house – the heavens!

Anything from God is good by itself, but when God now opens what He Himself calls **good treasure**, then you should be more excited over it than any rich family member's promise or promises. Dear reader, if you truly know God and have faith in Him, then you should begin to just thank Him and celebrate this good promise.

Pray this:

Father, I thank you for your love, mercy, and kindness over me. I thank you for opening up your good treasures, the heavens, upon my life. I thank you that due to your good treasures being opened upon my life, my life will not be stagnant. I will become a "showcase of your treasures," in Jesus' name.

2. You will enjoy maximum wellness, prosperity, and peace.

Our verse of consideration further says "to give rain to your land in its season." Rain, here, may mean the literal rain and everything people enjoy in a rainy season. It may also mean wellness, buoyancy, and peace. Your land, on the other hand, is anything belonging to you. So, this pronouncement here could refer to your "land" of health, marriage, career, business, etc.

Be sure to give special and careful attention to the expression, "In its seasons." Whenever anything operates out of its seasons, it can become chaotic or problematic. So, while it is a blessing in itself to enjoy rain, it is a greater blessing to enjoy it in its seasons, not outside of them.

Anything out of its seasons can be likened to fire taken out of its place. Fire in its place can cook food or warm a room, whereas fire out of the same place can cause destruction and hazards. I pray that good things will be in their right places, performing the right functions for you, and yielding good and right things into your life, at the right times, in Jesus' name.

Based on the verse in review, God says that when your heavens are opened, rain will fall for you in its seasons. Nothing good will be out of its place in your life. You will be blessed because everything and everyone in your life will be at the right place, doing right things, and achieving the right results.

Pray this:

Father, in the name of Jesus, rain will fall on all my lands - my land of health, my land of education, my land of finances, and every other land that I have. I decree, rain will fall at the right seasons into everything belonging to me; there shall be no more delays. When rain falls, it brings harvest. So, I decree and declare, no more dryness and drought in my life, career, marriage, and destiny. It is my season of seasons – a season that will usher me into continuous seasons of buoyancy, bliss, and breakthroughs, in Jesus' name.

Prayer Declarations

As you read this book, God's good treasure will open upon you. Rain will fall for you in its seasons. All the blessings attached to having rain will flow into your life. Whatever needs to grow in your life will grow. Whatever needs to produce good harvests will produce good harvests. Whoever needs to sow into your life will not withhold it. Helpers and facilitators will go extra miles to beautify your life. I decree that there will be no drought or dryness in your life. Everything and everyone will work well for you. Nothing will be out of place in your life; all things will be in place, yielding good results for you.

Due to these open heavens, you will have abundance of treasures and peace on all sides, in Jesus' name.

3. "Rain will fall upon your land."

When rain falls upon your land, your land will deliver back into your life the abundance locked up inside it. All blessings come from the ground – from what we eat to what we wear, drive, and use daily. When your heavens are opened, the ground will open for you all the treasures that will make your life blissful and peaceful. The best of the ground you tread upon will be released to you and your life will be an extraordinary one.

I pray that as you read this book, you will be among those who will eat the best of the land you dwell in. You will not eat crumbs or leftovers; the abundance of the seas and the lands shall be delivered to you, in Jesus' name. Due to your open heavens, even when you travel to other lands, the lands will yield their resources to you and everyone coming in contact with you will favor you and do you good, in Jesus' name.

The Israelites moved from places to places, but they enjoyed God's presence in every land, as long as they walked in obedience. Psalms 105:13-15 says, "When they went from one nation to another, From *one* kingdom to another people, He permitted no one to do them wrong; Yes, He rebuked kings for their sakes, *Saying,* "Do not touch My anointed ones, And do My prophets no harm."

Prayer Declarations

As the Israelites move from nation to nation and enjoyed God's open heavens, you will enjoy even better. As you read this book, the heavens will permanently open upon you. As you travel daily from your house and move from place to place during the course of the day, none will do you evil, none will wrong you, and none will work against you. Everyone will work together to give you what you need and desire. Whoever or whatever wants to stand in your way of progress will be rebuked and removed by God. You have become a "touch not" for evil, in Jesus' name. None will harm you, none will hurt you, none will touch you for evil, but all will hail you, help you, and honor you, in Jesus' name.

4. God will bless the "work of your hand."

When the work of someone's hand is blessed, it will not matter whether it's a small or large scale work or business – or whether you are a federal, city, or state employee – the person will enjoy sufficiency even while receiving meagre remuneration. There will always be a way. Grace will be released upon the "meagre" income, and as a result of your open heavens, the seemingly small income will be sufficient at each point of your life.

But then I want you to notice that the verse actually says that God will bless "all" the work of your hands. This means that work here is in multiple fold with layers of applications. For instance, if you are married, your marriage is a work, and it shall be blessed. Any project you have at hand right now is a "work," and it is blessed in Jesus' name. I pray that anything and everything that your hands embark upon will prosper.

Psalms 90:17 declares, "May the favor of the Lord our God rest on us; establish the work of our hands for us— yes, establish the work of our hands." The Lord will certainly bless your work, business and all you do. The beauty and favor of the lord will rest upon all your works. God will honor you and confirm and establish all the works of your hands, in Jesus name.

Prayer Declarations

Due to your open heavens, whatever work you have now will prosper. If you are looking to change work, due to your open heavens, many doors of job opportunities will open for you. If you don't have any job, I am in agreement with you now, based on Matthew 18:19, you will become gainfully employed. If you are looking to embark on a business, all resources needed are released for you now, in Jesus' name.

I decree, your heavens are opened. Your hands are blessed. The work of your hands are blessed. Whatever you lay your hands upon will prosper. Your health is blessed. Everything about you is blessed. You will move from strength to strength. You will not be weary but will mount up and abound in strength, in Jesus' name (Matthew 18:19; Psalms 1:3; Psalms 84:7).

5. "You will lend to many nations, but you will not borrow."

Due to ignorance and sometimes lack of faith, some believers don't set their minds and stretch their faith to believe this blessing. In the Bible, nations can represent many things. People are nations. A nation can also represent a place where people dwell in, a company, or any establishment run by people. In Genesis 25:23, God refers to two babies, Jacob and Esau, as "nations." So, when the verse says, you will lend to nations, it can mean lending to people or lending to nations, that is, different peoples of the world.

PRAYER DECLARATIONS

As a result of your reading this book, the Lord will bless you beyond measure. He will give you unquantifiable, unending, and unparalleled resources. You will have more than enough. Your blessings will overflow and you will be a lender and not a borrower. I pray that if you do borrow, it will be money that will give you uncommon assets and dividends, in Jesus' name.

ADDITIONAL BLESSINGS

Most of the major blessings that you will start to enjoy when your heavens are opened are presented as prayer points throughout this book. Aside from the ones already mentioned above, as contained in Deuteronomy 28:12, open heavens will make you enjoy one or more of the following:

- Supernatural power of God
- Spiritual manifestations of the gifts of the Holy Spirit
- Inexplicable joy
- Undeniable bliss
- Healings
- Divine visitations
- Divine instructions
- Clear knowledge of what to do at critical points in life
- Prosperity
- All-round wellness
- Miracles, signs and wonders
- Revivals
- Victories over haters and enemies
- Continuous divine interventions
- Absence of fear, even in the midst of chaos and storms
- Willingness of helpers and others to support you
- Daily guidance
- Absence of wars, afflictions, and evil reports.

- Empowerment to succeed
- The land you live in will favor you; you will not eat crumbs of the land.
- Blessings of God will overtake you
- God will honor you and people will be afraid to hurt you
- You will be blessed in the work of your hands
- Abiding presence of God
- Unhindered access to all the treasures in God's presence
- Promotion from God
- Abundance of the seas will be delivered to you

You can formulate daily prayers, using the above listed blessings. For instance, you can pray this:

- Father, in the name of Jesus, as I step out today, the heavens are opened upon my life. Lord, intervene in my life. Let me be met with favor everywhere I go today. Everyone will favor me. All my endeavors will be successful and I will come back home rejoicing, in Jesus' name.

- In name of Jesus, on this day, I enjoy the benefit of protection. No weapon fashioned against me will prosper. God will arise and destroy anybody trying to hurt me or harm me, in Jesus' name.

- In the name of Jesus, the heavens are opened upon

me. I enjoy God's presence today and all the treasures from God's presence will follow me throughout the day. In the presence of God, there is no sickness or evil; therefore, I reject all forms of sicknesses and whatever evil that is flying around will not come near me, in Jesus' name.

Prayer Declarations

I declare that the heavens are opened over you. God will intervene in your life. Whatever is presently going in the wrong direction in your life will turn around to favor you. As a result of these open heavens, your enemies will be defeated and destroyed before you. God will be a shield of protection around you day and night. Anybody attempting to injure you in your sleep will fall into his or her own destruction and wickedness. God will arise on your behalf. He will lift you above all your enemies. He will fill your mouth with laughter and your life with peace, in Jesus' name.

PART 2
BENEFICIARIES OF OPEN HEAVENS

5
UPLIFTING ENCOUNTERS

Since this part of our discussion is centered on the chronicles of beneficiaries of open heavens in the Scripture, each of the subsequent chapters will be used to explore the experiences of these people. The goal is to make us relive these experiences with them and to position us to receive even greater dimensions of open heavens in all areas of our own lives.

Indeed, from Adam in the book of Genesis to Apostle John in Revelation, the Bible is filled with men and women of God who enjoyed God's open heavens. For example, Apostle John narrated his experience in Revelation 4:1, "After this I looked, and behold, a door standing open in heaven! And the first voice which I had heard, like *the sound* of a [war] trumpet speaking with me, said, "Come up here, and I will show you what must take place after these things."

The apostle, in this particular encounter, practically saw the heavens opened up. In a vision, he heard specific instructions and was shown mysteries that would still happen in the future.

Pray this:

Father, in the name of Jesus, as I step out this day, this week and this month, let your heavens open over me. Show me the things to come that will make the journey of my life beautiful. I will not walk in darkness. My eyes will see clearly and I will know what to do. Anoint my ears to hear specific instructions that will lift me up spiritually, mentally, and financially, in Jesus' name.

Beyond Scriptural References

It is cheering to know that, apart from those who experienced open heavens in the Bible, various people have experienced open heavens in contemporary times; and, of course, people will continue to experience open heavens till the end of age. Even for the biblical allusions, only few people's experiences can be examined in detail.

For those that will establish the focus of our discussions in the subsequent chapters, each person's experience will be summarized, and there will be different parameters of prayers such as general prayers, declarations prayers, and personalized prayers. I urge you to take these prayers seriously, as every one of them is Holy Spirit inspired and generated. You should pray these prayers personally for your life (health, career, business, ministry, finances etc.), spouse, children, immediate family, extended family, church family, colleagues, etc., as you are led by the Holy Spirit.

It is an undisputable fact that what you watch and read always leaves deposits in your life. So, get ready! As you read the experiences in the next few chapters and pray the accompanying prayers, the floodgates of heavens will burst open upon your life. It's surely a new day and a new season in your life!

Pray this:

I decree and declare that as exile could not stop Apostle John's divine assignment and he was still empowered and commissioned by God to write the book of Revelation, nothing will be able to frustrate my destiny. I command whatever is holding my life down to break right now. I decree that there will be no exile, no limitation, and no barrier in my life. I break free from every hold and I am empowered by the Holy Spirit to be who God has called me to be. I will also do what God has apportioned me to do in this land of the living, in Jesus' name (Revelation 1:9; 4:1).

Prayer Declarations

I pray and decree that what should have been working, but has not worked up till now in your life will start to work. The good things stolen will be returned. Great things, including relationships and good opportunities that you have missed, will come back to you. Heavens will open wide upon you and you will have testimonies, good reports, and great fulfillments, in Jesus' name.

6
NOAH: UNCOMMON FAVOR FROM OPEN HEAVENS

As recorded in the book of Genesis, Noah had open heavens experiences. Genesis 6:8 says, "But Noah found favor in the eyes of the Lord." Also, in Genesis 7: 10-12, it is recorded, "And after the seven days [God released the rain and] the floodwaters came on the earth. In the six hundredth year of Noah's life, on the seventeenth day of the second month, on that same day all the fountains of the great deep [subterranean waters] burst open, and the windows and floodgates of the heavens were opened. It rained on the earth for forty days and forty nights."

What we find in these verses is that among the people of his time, Noah encountered God, and the heavens opened upon his world. The result was that the fountains of the great deep burst open; the windows of heaven also opened, while the floodgates were unleashed. Now, the most interesting part is that each of these elements was recorded in the plural form – fountains, windows and floodgates, which makes it clear that with open heavens, there is always an overflow from God.

IMPACTS OF OPEN HEAVENS ON NOAH

Here are some points to note about Noah's open heaven experience:

- Noah was favored by God and was selected in the whole world of his time.

- The same heavens opened upon Noah and the people of his time; yet they were destroyed and he was preserved. He was selected by favor and preserved, while others were destroyed.

- People were making fun of him as he constructed the ark, most likely because he was in an environment where rainfall was unusual or non-existent (Genesis 2:6; Hebrews 11:6).

- Noah's open heavens experience happened after the fall of man. This means that, as at the time he entered the ark, some dangerous animals that could have harmed him also followed him into the ark! How did animals, including lions and snakes follow Noah after the fall of man? The Lord motivated them! It was the same God who stirred up the hearts of Zerubbabel, the priest, the governor, and the people to build His temple.

Pray this:

Lord God, stir up both animate and inanimate objects to advance and lift my destiny, in Jesus' name. What harms others will arm me; what hurts others, will help me, and what destroys others, will develop and lift me up, in Jesus' name.

God did not tell Noah to go into the ark; rather He told him to "come" into the ark (Genesis 7:1). This means God went ahead of him into the ark.

PRAYER DECLARATIONS

Wherever you go on this day and whatever you are going to do, God has gone ahead of you. Nobody will do you evil, all will do you good, in Jesus' name. As Noah found favor with God, favor is released upon your life. Wherever you go to today, you will not be rejected and you will not be hated by anybody. God's favor will flavor your life. Your heart desires shall be granted and you will return with testimonies, in Jesus' name.

I decree, in Jesus name, whatever benefit is due you will not be withheld from you. By the force of favor, you will receive all your benefits and there shall be a release of showers of blessings upon you, in Jesus' name.

BEGINNING OF FAVOR FOR NOAH

Genesis 5:28-29 says, "When Lamech had lived 182 years, he had a son. He named him Noah and said, "He will comfort us in the labor and painful toil of our hands caused by the ground the LORD has cursed."

What this passage reveals is that the favor that Noah experienced was the prophetic fulfilment of the meaning of his name 600 years after he was so named. His father, Lamech, had declared that Noah would bring rest and comfort to the ground that God had cursed. Truly, Noah became the link between the first world and the second world. God used Noah to bring rest and comfort back to the world after the other world was destroyed.

As it usually is with the things of God, it was a good thing that the prophetic declaration over Noah took as long as 600 years to come to full manifestation. The merciful God was simply giving the people enough time to repent from their wicked ways. However, as believers under a much better covenant, we can always pray for speedy fulfilment of God's promises and prophetic declarations in our lives.

Pray this:

- In the name of Jesus, I bind every spirit of delay of my blessings. I receive the grace of longevity, but I reject delay of prophetic declarations and plans of God for my life. Unlike Lamech's prophetic declaration over Noah that took 600 years, all of God's plans and spiritual prophetic declarations over my life shall be speedily delivered.

- I declare, in Jesus' name:
- No more delayed blessings
- No more going round in circles
- No more failures at the edges of breakthroughs
- No more "almost made it" syndromes
- (Genesis 5;29, Matthew 16:19, Jeremiah 29:11, Deuteronomy 2:3)

- I decree over my life, I am in my season of open heavens. All my breakthroughs shall be delivered on the wings of angels. As the couriers of Suza rode on the king's relay horses to speedily deliver good news on behalf of the Jews (Esther 8:14), angelic couriers of heavens will spread favor over my name and destiny. Anywhere I go today, everyone and everything will work in my favor. Helpers of destiny will go extra miles to make my life comfortable and beautiful, in Jesus' name.

- It is written in Esther 8:11, "In it the king granted the Jews who were in every city the right to assemble and to defend their lives; to destroy, to kill, and to annihilate any armed force that might attack them, their little children, and women; and to take the enemies' goods as plunder." The King of kings has given me the authority to tread upon serpents and scorpions and I have authority over all powers of darkness and nothing will by any means hurt me (Luke 10:19). After these orders, in this my season of open heavens, I shoot down and render useless every power of darkness trying to touch me or any of my family members. I command sicknesses and affliction of the body trying to hinder my destiny, lose your grip and come out of my body and the body of my loved ones, in Jesus' name!

SAFETY THROUGH OPEN HEAVENS

During the time God was to destroy the old evil world, it was said of Noah and his household: "On the very same day Noah and Noah's sons, Shem, Ham, and Japheth, and Noah's wife and the three wives of his sons with them, entered the ark…all flesh died that moved on the earth: birds and cattle and beasts and every creeping thing that creeps on the earth, and every man. All in whose nostrils was the breath of the spirit of life, all that was on the dry land, died. So He destroyed all living things which were on the face of the ground: both man and cattle, creeping thing and bird of the air. They were destroyed from the earth. Only Noah and those who were with him in the ark remained alive" (Genesis 7:13-23). It was a wonderful testimony of safety amid widespread destruction. This is one of the blessings that Noah enjoyed through open heavens, and it should be your portion too.

Pray this:

As Noah and his family entered the ark and were saved and preserved, I prophetically pronounce over my life, anywhere I go today becomes the ark of safety for me. I am saved and preserved. I decree that in this season of open heavens, my loved ones and I are saved and preserved. As we travel by air, road, or rail, we are saved and preserved. Wherever our feet treads becomes the ark of safety because of us. As the people with Noah were saved, so is everyone that will be with me and around me; they will be saved, protected and preserved, in Jesus' name.

PRAYER DECLARATIONS

- Flood is not limited to waters and rain. Floods represent catastrophic conditions and events beyond a person's control. I decree and declare that you will enjoy peace like a river throughout this day, week, month, and year, in Jesus' name. I decree peace of God in your health, relationships, career, and all other areas. There shall be no storm or any flood-like event in your life and the places you will tread upon, in Jesus' name.

- All the animals were motivated by God and they followed Noah into the ark. God will motivate everything and everyone you need to advance your destiny; they will travel extra miles and work tirelessly for your progress.

- As the animals walked two by two into the ark, all the resources you need will come to you in multiples. Uncompleted projects will be completed speedily.

Abandoned projects will kick off to the finish line. Grace to start new and amazing things in your world is released upon you, in Jesus' name.

PERSONALIZED PRAYERS FOR OPEN HEAVENS

Genesis 7:10-12 declares, "And it came to pass after seven days that the waters of the flood were on the earth. In the six hundredth year of Noah's life, in the second month, the seventeenth day of the month, on that day all the fountains of the great deep were broken up, and the windows of heaven were opened. And the rain was on the earth forty days and forty nights."

It is said here that the heavens opened and God released the rain; and it rained on the earth for forty days and forty nights.

Pray this:

- In the name of Jesus, after the order of the above scriptures, let heavens open upon my life, spouse, children, family members (mention names), ministry, business, career, finances, and health (add more, where necessary).

- I declare, no more dryness or drought in my life. I decree showers of blessings and peace like a river. As rain brings comfort and causes earth to release its treasures to everyone connected to God, so today...

(Mention names) will experience open heavens and there shall be testimonies, in Jesus' name.

- I reject all manners of delay; I break the hold of spirits of delays in my life. I affirm God's plans over my life and the lives of my loved ones. Nothing good will be delayed in our lives anymore. God's promises and plans will come to pass speedily in our lives. As all the animals followed Noah into the ark, goodness, mercy, favor, grace will follow me into my prepared blessings on this day, in Jesus name.

- I pray and declare that, this is the day the Lord has made for me. It is a day of peace, a day of joy, a day of good reports, and pleasant surprises. There may be floods of troubles in the world, but I am in Christ, my Ark of Safety. No trouble will come near my family. No plague will come near us throughout this day. I decree the peace of God over every one of us. My family members and I will experience showers of blessings on this day of the Lord, in Jesus' name.

Follow the above prayers with the hymn, "There Shall Be Showers of Blessing." I'm delighted to inform you that the Holy Spirit sang this song into my spirit, using the same tune, but with slightly different words. I'd like to share this modified version with you. If you don't know the original hymn, you can Google it or watch it on YouTube. You can familiarize yourself with the tune, and then sing it using the lyrics given to me by the Holy Spirit. It goes this way:

Showers of blessings are falling upon me and my …(business, family, friends…)

These are the seasons of refreshing, pouring from the Savior above.

Showers of blessings, showers of blessings are here,

Unending blessings are flowing from our Father above.

Unending treasures are flowing from our Father above.

Unending breakthroughs are pouring from our Father above.

As you sing this song daily, you will experience what you are singing and confessing.

Proverbs 18:21 says, "Death and life are in the power of the tongue, And those who love it will eat its fruit." My understanding of this scripture as explained to me by the Holy Spirit is: Every seed generates fruits. And the second part of the verse mentions "fruit." The question, then, is where is the seed that should normally come before fruit? That seed is the word you speak or the song you sing. So, whatever comes from your tongue is a seed that carries the "gene" of power to cause death or life, depending on whether the word is negative or positive. If the word is positive, you will reap fruits of positive things, and if the words are negatives, the fruits also will be negative.

So, as you sing the "Showers of Blessings" chorus, as rephrased by the Holy Spirit, you are sowing positive words loaded in the song into your life and future. Your seeds sown through the song will definitely bring back uncountable harvests of fruits into your life and whoever and whatever you sing the song upon.

Sing the rephrased chorus of this song daily. Let it become a part of your thoughts. Instead of thinking negative things, such as thoughts of defeats, deaths, sicknesses, and fears, sing the rephrased chorus every time and get ready – your showers of blessings will definitely be released, in Jesus' name.

Please, note that the above advice was inspired the Holy Spirit Himself. He said to me to advise every reader of this book to sing that rephrased chorus anytime Satan is suggesting fears, worries, defeats, deaths, and other negative thoughts into their minds. So, whenever Satan begins to play such tricks on your mind, just begin to sing, for example: *Showers of blessings are falling upon me and my children…* (Or anything or anyone Satan wants you to think evil over).

You can reword the song further by mentioning names. In my case, for instance, I can sing it over all my children, grandchildren and my entire lineage:

> *Showers of blessings are falling upon the ADEYEYES,*
> *Showers of blessings are falling upon me and my children*
> *These are the seasons of refreshing, pouring from Savior above.*
> *Showers of blessings, showers of blessings are here,*
> *Unending blessings are flowing from our father above.*
> *Unending treasures are flowing from our father above.*
> *Unending breakthroughs are flowing from our father above*

As you sing this song over your business, your loved ones and everything about you, there shall be unending testimonies, miracles, signs, and wonders experienced by the ones you sing over, in Jesus' name.

EXALTATION AND VICTORY THROUGH OPEN HEAVENS

The word says in Genesis 7:17-23, "Now the flood was on the earth forty days. The waters increased and lifted up the ark, and it rose high above the earth. The waters prevailed and greatly increased on the earth, and the ark moved about on the surface of the waters. And the waters prevailed exceedingly on the earth, and all the high hills under the whole heaven were covered. The waters prevailed fifteen cubits upward, and the mountains were covered. And all flesh died that moved on the earth: birds and cattle and beasts and every creeping thing that creeps on the earth, and every man. All in whose nostrils was the breath of the spirit of life, all that was on the dry land, died. So He destroyed all living things which were on the face of the ground: both man and cattle, creeping thing and bird of the air."

Pray this:

- As the waters increased and lifted up the ark, and it floated [high] above the land, God will lift me and everything I lay my hands upon. God will take me to the high places of life. I will not peck the floors. I will not eat crumbs of the floor but the best of this land, in Jesus' name.

- As I step out today, as the waters lifted and floated the ark, I receive fresh anointing to lift and showcase my destiny. The waters of life will not swallow me, but will showcase and make me, my children, business, and ministry (add more) to be visible for affirmation, promotion, distinction, and coronation, in Jesus' name.

- The waters prevailed greatly and all living things on the earth perished. Oh God my heavenly Father, this day is the day you have made, it shall do me good. Whatever is programmed to prevail and cause people to perish will promote me.

- I pray in the name of Jesus, as Noah and his family prevailed over the waters that killed others, I decree that what is dangerous out there today is under my feet and the feet of my family members.

- In the name of Jesus, what kills and subdues people of my gender, age, and time will submit to me. What overcomes and overpowers people in my family will be subdued by me. What sinks others will be my stepping stone to my shining and rising, in Jesus' name.

- In Genesis 7: 23, only those who were with Noah survived. All those who were with Paul in Acts 27: 44 survived the shipwreck. Oh God, my heavenly Father, I pray this day that all my family members, all those who are connected to me, all those who will be in the same means of transportation with me, will be saved because of me. There will be no accident. There will be no emergencies and no evil report. All things will go well for everyone connected to me, in Jesus' name.

Distinguishing Grace through Open Heavens

Genesis 6: 5-16 reads, "Then the Lord saw that the wickedness of man was great in the earth, and that every intent of the thoughts of his heart was only evil continually. And the Lord was sorry that He had made man on the earth, and He was grieved in His heart. So the Lord said, "I will destroy man whom I have created from the face of the earth, both man and beast, creeping thing and birds of the air, for I am sorry that I have made them." But Noah found grace in the eyes of the Lord. This is the genealogy of Noah. Noah was a just man, perfect in his generations. Noah walked with God. And Noah begot three sons: Shem, Ham, and Japheth. The earth also was corrupt before God, and the earth was filled with violence. So God looked upon the earth, and indeed it was corrupt; for all flesh had corrupted their way on the earth. And God said to Noah, "The end of all flesh has come before Me, for the earth is filled with violence through them; and behold, I will destroy them with the earth. Make yourself an ark of gopherwood; make rooms in the ark, and cover it inside and outside with pitch. And this is how you shall make it: The length of the ark shall be three hundred cubits, its width fifty cubits, and its height thirty cubits. You shall make a window for the ark, and you shall finish it to a cubit from above; and set the door of the ark in its side. You shall make it with lower, second, and third decks."

Despite the rampant moral and spiritual corruption on the earth during the time of Noah, Noah received grace to live a distinctly righteous life before God. This positioned him to be a useful vessel of honor to God and an instrument of salvation to himself, his loved ones, and all other creatures that entered the ark with him.

Pray this:

- On this day, the thoughts of my heart, my actions, and reactions will please the Lord.

- I receive grace to put my mind and imagination to great use. Innovative and creative thinking will fill my mind, in Jesus' name.

- God will not regret over me. God will not be sorry for creating and saving me. God will not regret blessing me and keeping me alive. I will use everything God has given me to promote His kingdom today and all the days of my life, in Jesus' name.

In the midst of wickedness, Noah found favor. On this day, as I move from place to place, I will be met with favor and grace. God will favor me and everything created by God will honor me, grace me, favor me, and help to beautify my destiny. Grace makes great; I will become greater and will not diminish today, in all areas of my life.

- Father, I pray that I will walk in habitual fellowship with you. Teach me to take your presence everywhere I will go today. As Noah increased and became the father of three sons, this day, this week, this month, and this year, I decree that I will not diminish in strength, wisdom, and in all good things. I will become everything good you have created me to become, in Jesus' name.

- Father, I decree and declare that despite the moral and spiritual bankruptcy in the world today, I will be your light and ambassador everywhere I go today, in Jesus' name. I will not fail, fall, nor falter. I will not miss God's true direction for my life.

- In Jesus name, I will not walk another person's walk, run another person's race. I receive grace to stay focus and stay in my line. I will be a great achiever and an uncommon trailblazer, in Jesus name.

- As Noah received insights from the Lord to construct an ark that he did not see with the physical eyes, Father, anoint my eyes of understanding. Help me to see, hear, and do what the Holy Spirit is showing and speaking to me, in Jesus' name.

- Noah was a blessing to everyone and everything in the ark, because he understood what God wanted him to construct. My Lord, and my God, breathe upon me, upon my inner man, help me to have clarity and understanding, help me to know what to do that will set me high on the hill and be a blessing to the world, in Jesus name.

- Lord, Moses constructed the tabernacle for you in the book of Exodus, Noah built an ark to your specifications, Nehemiah and Ezra repaired the broken walls of Jerusalem, Solomon built the temple for you. Today, I receive ideas, innovation, and wisdom to build and make significant changes that will attract nations to you, in Jesus' name.

- I will not be ordinary. I refuse to do ordinary things and to achieve ordinary results. Since your Spirit lives in me, I refuse to be a mere person on this day. I receive supernatural enablement to make me think, create, and achieve extraordinary results that will positively change my world, in Jesus name.

DIVINE REMEMBRANCE THROUGH OPEN HEAVENS

Genesis 8:1 states, "And God remembered *and* thought kindly of Noah and every living thing and all the animals that were with him in the ark; and God made a wind blow over the land, and the waters receded."

PRAYER DECLARATIONS

- God remembered Noah and caused a wind to blow and the waters of destruction receded. As you have read this book to this point, God's wind will blow over your destiny; whatever represents evil waters in your life must dry off right now, in Jesus' name.

- This wind of God will blow away from your life, evil symptoms, evil people, evil circumstances, and all evil occurrences, in Jesus' name.

- When God remembered Noah, what was a problem was removed from his life. God remembered Sarah and bareness was removed from her life (Genesis 30:22). God remembered the covenant He made with Abraham, Isaac, and Jacob; and He removed His people from slavery and captivity of over 400 years (Exodus 2:24). God remembered Hannah and He opened her womb (1 Samuel 1:19). I decree and declare over you, as God remembered all these people and took positive actions to solve their longstanding problems, there shall be a turnaround in your life. All your longstanding problems will turn into solutions and celebrations, in Jesus' name.

- God will open His heavens upon you. As He remembered Noah and he came out of the ark, you will come out of every pit, every problem, every captivity, and every difficulty, in Jesus' name. Whoever and whatever has been your ark of safety will not become a net or hole to hold you captive.

- I decree and declare upon you that the grace of right timing is released upon your destiny, upon your family, and upon your career. God told Noah to enter the ark in Genesis 7:1, and He told him to go out of the ark in Genesis 8: 16. In Jesus' name, you will not miss your time and moments. The grace of right timing is upon you to do the right things at the right times of your life, with the right people, in the right places, and you will obtain right results, in Jesus' name.

7

EZEKIEL: SUPERNATURAL VISITATIONS THROUGH OPEN HEAVENS

Ezekiel was one of the major prophets of the Old Testament. His first open heavens experience is found in the first chapter of this book. He had many supernatural encounters as a result of this experience. Here is how he narrated what happened: *"Now it came to pass in the thirtieth year, in the fourth month, on the fifth day of the month, as I was among the captives by the River Chebar, that the heavens were opened and I saw visions of God. On the fifth day of the month, which was in the fifth year of King Jehoiachin's captivity, the word of the Lord came expressly to Ezekiel the priest, the son of Buzi, in the land of the Chaldeans by the River Chebar; and the hand of the Lord was upon him there"* (Ezekiel 1:1-3).

While Ezekiel was in captivity among other captives, the heavens opened above him. Some Bible commentators believe that Ezekiel was 30 years old when he had this remarkable experience. This was the age when priests, after years of preparation, would step into the full swing of their callings as priests over God's people. Unfortunately, at this time, there was no altar, no synagogue (church), and no freedom for Ezekiel to carry out his kingdom assignment.

Ezekiel was not even a free man, not to talk of being used as a priest to free others. To the natural mind, it was over for Ezekiel – a slave among other slaves. Someone who should have been a leader in his own country was in bondage - helpless, fruitless, and hopeless in a strange country!

My beloved, it is possible to be in the lowest of the lowest valleys of life and things may be going haywire and really bad. It is possible that your life did not go as you planned and hoped for it to be. It is possible to be in the lowest of the lowest valleys of no money, poor health, and "all-rounder" lowest of life. I call this kind of experience "valley of the shadow of death" experience.

If you are presently on the mountain top experience of life (Good times, great life, and all-round buoyancy), I implore you to love and appreciate God daily. He is your Helper, who helped in taking you to the "mountain top" lifestyle. You should also maximize your position by praying daily for others who may be in the valley of valleys and valleys of shadows of death conditions in life.

However, it is also possible that as a believer, you may be going through one or more of life's situations such as:

- No spouse yet
- No child to call your own yet
- No family support
- No trustworthy friend
- No good health
- No financial support
- No emotional support
- No meaningful thing going on in your life
- No progress
- No hope
- No help
- No legal documents (If you are not in your country of birth)
- Nobody to connect you to people in high places.

Whatever situation it may be that makes you feel you are in an "all-rounder valley of the shadows of deaths" experience, God of open heavens will intervene and give you an "open heavens" experience that will cancel all your years of labor, struggling and toiling. I can certainly share many more stories of my "valley of valleys" and "valley of shadows of death" experiences with you, but I just want you to know that the God of open heavens, who inspired me to write this book, will lift you from whatever valley you are in. In Jesus' name, God will lift you from every pit of life, every storm of life, and from every valley of the shadow of death to your own mountain top experiences of life. God, who selected Ezekiel among others, opened heavens above him and gave him assignments to the people, will select you, open His heavens above you, and cause you to rise above where you currently are, in Jesus' name

Let me share some prayer points the Holy Spirit downloaded into my spirit as I read the above verses from Ezekiel 1 in the following series of insights and prayer bullets.

Pray this:

Oh God my heavenly Father, as you visited Ezekiel and still used him as a Prophet, despite captivity, change my status – my financial status, spiritual status, marital status (if you are single). Move me from grace to grace, and from glory to glory, in Jesus' name (2 Corinthians 3:18).

Ezekiel could not function in the office of a priest because of wrong location, wrong label, wrong timing; but God re-arranged things and God used him as a Prophet to the Israelites.

Pray this:

My father and my God, the all-powerful, all knowing, all seeing, and all-present God, after the order of

Ezekiel, re-order and re-align my life, compensate for my inadequacies, weaknesses, failures, and mistakes. As Ezekiel's destiny was not useless and not wasted and as he was still able to serve in the same high capacity of a prophet instead of a priest, I decree and declare that my life, my destiny, my career will not operate below my God-ordained destiny and God—ordained plans, in Jesus' name. I receive grace to function in high dimensions of life, in Jesus' name.

If the nation had not gone into captivity, Ezekiel was supposed to have been a priest; still, God lifted him from being a priest to prophet in a strange land. Amos was a shepherd, but God lifted him to be a prophet, despite opposition (Amos 7: 14 -15).

Pray this:

No matter the storms, negativities, and oppositions of life, I will not be unfruitful or unproductive. God, who lifted Amos from a shepherd to a prophet will lift me to operate in His dimensions. I receive grace to do good and great things God has packaged me to do. I will manifest and deliver what God has sent me into the world to do, in Jesus' name.

DECLARE AS FOLLOWS:

- I am not useless
- I will be who God has called me to be

- I will step into the levels God wants me to step into
- I will do what God has packaged me to do
- I will go where God wants me to go
- I will speak and declare what God has deposited in me
- I will create and invent all the things God has packaged into my destiny
- I will not go backwards; I will move forward in life
- I will not crawl in the race of life
- I will not be slow, nor be behind in destiny
- I will fly like the eagles in destiny and
- I will take my right places in destiny,
- My life will be useful, peaceful, impactful, and fruitful, in Jesus name.

Romans 8:19; Jeremiah 1:5; Jeremiah 7:24; Psalms 84:7.

Renewed Strength from Open Heavens

If you are an older reader, this is for you. There is no age barrier, education barrier, or any other barrier that can stop God from helping you to fulfil your destiny. It is never too late for anybody in Christ. The grace of God can erase the errors and mistakes of your past. God's heavens will open upon your life, and you will make up for lost years and lost opportunities, in Jesus' name.

Pray this:

God will visit and open His special treasures and His heavens upon my life. After the order of Moses that stepped into the calling of God at age 80 (Exodus 7:7), I prophesy upon my life, it is not too late for me. Whatever promise of God that has eluded me is speedily restored and released back into my life. I regain lost grounds and lost opportunities, in Jesus' name.

God called Moses at 80, Aaron at 83 years, and Caleb was still strong to fight and possess the lands God gave him at 85 years. These great men stepped into God's callings and started great things in their lives at the ages people would have labeled them as "old." This same God will give you good surprises too. Whatever you have been waiting to do and has not happened until now, due to God's open heavens upon you, great things will suddenly be happening in your life. The anointing to be successful at any age is released upon you, in Jesus name. All the resources you have always needed but have never materialized will suddenly come together, step-by-step in your life. I prophesy a shifting of things. Showers of blessings are falling on you to bring all these resources, in Jesus' name (Exodus 7:7, Joshua 14: 10 -11, Ezekiel 34:26).

UNCOMMON LIFTING THROUGH OPEN HEAVENS

This is especially for younger people. There is nobody too young to step into the divine will of God. Biblical scholars calculated Samuel's age at about eleven years old, when God called him (1 Samuel 3:4). Joseph received his first dream at about 17 years old and was 30 years old when he stood before Pharaoh (Genesis 41:46). David killed Goliath as a youth and started reigning as a king at age 30. (1 Samuel 17: 23; 2 Samuel 5:4). Uzziah was 16 years old when he became a king (2 Chronicles 26:1).

All these great men were very young when they answered the callings of God and stepped into their places in destiny. Children and youths from Christian homes are not too young to do exploits for the Lord. God expects our children and youths to yield their hearts to Him and know Him for themselves. God said Abraham would teach his children to know Him.

Pray this:

- Father, in the name of Jesus, let your heavens open upon my children and all youths in the body of Christ. As David, Joseph, and Samuel stepped into the work of God, my children will be mighty vessels in God's hands.

- My children will not be left behind in the things of God. Lord, give them new hearts that are tender, sensitive, and responsive to your touch. Imprint your words into their innermost thoughts and give them quick understanding. Let your mighty hands uproot childishness, lack of spiritual seriousness, and worldliness from their lives. (Ezekiel 1:19; Hebrews 8:10).

- I cover my children in the blood of Jesus. As they go back and forth, none will trouble them, nor make them afraid. The grace to take bold steps and to do great exploits at young ages is released upon them. My children will not miss their great moments in life. Father, remove bad friends and negative influencers around them. Release the "anointing of rightness" upon them. I decree and declare that they will be right on schedules with all the schedules of God for their lives, in Jesus name (Revelation 12:11; Daniel 11:32b).

As a parent, ensure to pray the above prayers for your babies and teach the younger ones the ways of God from when your children start to talk.

Fruit of the Womb from Open Heavens

Due to the burden I carry for couples believing God for children, in one of God's supernatural visitations to my family, He gave me an anointing to lay hands on women who are waiting to have children. God said as they connect by faith, He will terminate their frustrations. I remember sharing this visitation at a church in Houston, where I had been invited to minister many years ago. I remember praying for a lady and she conceived within the same month.

If you are believing God for children, as you lay this page

on your navel area daily and connect to God by faith, I pray that the God of open heavens will break every hold of delay and will visit you with the children of your heart desires, in Jesus' name.

Pray this:

- Father in heaven, open your heavens over my life. Children are one of the treasures of your presence; release into my womb children that will love you and propagate your work on earth.

- As you graciously remembered Sarah and fulfilled your promise of Isaac, send my own Isaacs.

- As you remembered Rachel, opened her womb and made her to conceive an uncommon, destined child, open my womb and cause me to conceive uncommon children that will bear the lights for others to tread, Jesus' name.

- As you remembered Hannah, remember me Lord, and cause me to conceive and deliver children that will leave remarkable and undeniable imprints in the lives of mankind, in Jesus name (Genesis 21:1, 30;22; 1 Samuel 1: 19, 20)

Prayer Declarations

The Lord visited Ezekiel while he was a slave, in a strange land. Your turn for a supernatural visitation is now. It's your season of visitations, wherever you are, geographically, in the world. Whether you still reside in your country of birth or not, it's your turn for open heavens. No matter what your status is, you are about to enter new seasons of your life that will demarcate and showcase you with God's glory, in Jesus' name.

8
BLESSINGS FROM EZEKIEL'S OPEN HEAVENS

Let us examine the five blessings that followed Ezekiel after this awesome experience of open heavens! As we do so, we will raise prayer points from these experiences. I pray that such blessings will follow you too, in Jesus' name.

Ezekiel 1: 1- 3 reveals these blessings: "Now it came to pass in the thirtieth year, in the fourth month, on the fifth day of the month, as I was among the captives by the River Chebar, that the heavens were opened and I saw visions of God. On the fifth day of the month, which was in the fifth year of King Jehoiachin's captivity, the word of the Lord came expressly to Ezekiel the priest, the son of Buzi, in the land of the Chaldeans by the River Chebar; and the hand of the Lord was upon him there."

The blessings are:

1. He received supernatural selection for favor among other captives – verse 1
2. He saw special visions of God – verse 1
3. He received God's word - verse 3
4. God's word went to him expressly – verse 3
5. The hand of God rested upon him – verse 3

SUPERNATURAL SELECTION BY GOD FOR FAVOR

Despite the fact that he was in captivity among other Israelites in Babylonia, God opened the heavens above Ezekiel **only**. The second line of this verse reads, "While I was **among the exiles** beside the River Chebar."

Dear reader, did you see that? Ezekiel was a captive among other captives from the nation of Israel. While he was among other people, he was the only one selected by God for an assignment. Ezekiel was singled out among others to see and to know secrets kept by God from other people of his time. This goes to show that a person can be singled out of a group, a crowd, or a family, and can encounter God in an open heavens experience. May God single you out for favor and for lifting, in Jesus' name.

My beloved, God can single you out for open heavens experience. He can single you out to enjoy benefits that others around you are not enjoying. The people around you will just observe these blessings of God upon you.

Moreover, rest assured that that no matter your marital status, qualifications, or career, God can and will single you out for open heavens experience. God can single you out by favor and can open His heavens upon you and give you multimillion dollar ideas, concepts, and innovations that will change the world forever! God can connect you with helpers of destinies, facilitators of events of life, and financiers of projects, thereby changing your life positively forever!

Here is a testimony to illustrate this. A Christian brother, who is a relative, happens to be very wealthy in the country of his birth – a place where his counterparts are eating from garbage cans and some are struggling to make ends meet. How did this happen? He testified that he experienced open heavens from God one fateful day. On that particular day, the Holy Spirit came upon him like a cloud and spoke to him about the business that would enrich him forever! He said the Holy Spirit mentioned his name and instructed him to go into this particular business, and that if he obeyed, he would enjoy forever. But if he disobeyed, he would have himself to blame forever. This relative is so rich that believers and unbelievers doing the same business as he does cannot rival him in excellence and wealth. Beloved, it is your turn to be favored.

Pray this:

- Father, in the name of Jesus, after the order of Ezekiel,

single me out for favor in my geographical location, in my profession, in my family, among my peers, and my counterparts. Lord, you are not a partial God and you change not. What you do for one, you can do for others, surround me with favor, like a shield.

- Lord, open your heavens above me. Download into my mind – ideas, concepts, and innovations that will rule the world. In Jesus name, Father, connect me with facilitators, financiers, and faithful people who will work extra hard, go extra miles, and supply all the "extras" I need to make me extra special, in my family, as well as my local and global environments, in Jesus name. (Ezekiel 1:1; Malachi 3:6; Hebrews 13:8; Psalms 5:12; Jeremiah 1:5)

- Father, in the name of Jesus, select me by your favor. David was selected by favor, out of his brothers, to be the king. Joseph was selected out of his eleven brothers by favor. Mary was chosen among other virgins. By favor, the widow of Zarephath was selected over other widows, to be fed and provided for. Lord, after these orders, select me among others. Let your favor lift me as you lifted David from the back of the desert. I will rule and reign and not be a mere person in my generation. I will be fed and provided for, no matter the economic conditions of my world.

- By God's grace, as Mary conceived and delivered by the power of the Holy Spirit, what God has packaged in me will be delivered and not aborted, in Jesus' name. (1 Samuel 16: 11- 12; Genesis 37:7; Luke 1:28; 1 Kings 17:16; Matthew 1:20 -21)

- Lord, by favor, you chose Jacob over Esau. As I step out this day, let your favor follow me, select me, introduce me and distinguish me everywhere I go. John said that Jesus was preferred above him. In Jesus name, I will be favored and preferred over others. I ask for this kind of 'preferential favor' to be upon my family, business and… (mention whatever you need God's preferential favor upon). Myself and everyone connected to me shall be preferred, have priorities over others, and be selected this day, in Jesus' name. (Romans 9: 9-12; John 1:30)

- Oh Lord, my heavenly Father, flavor my life, home, and family with your favor. By favor, Apostle Paul, the one killing believers, was promoted over other disciples. Zerah was supposed to come before Pharez, but by favor, Pharez broke through and was promoted to come first. My Lord and my God, in your favor, promote me. Promote the work of my hands and my family members. Anoint my head and the heads of my loved ones with your oil of promotion. Wherever we go today, we shall have priorities over others, be selected, and be promoted, in Jesus' name. By favor, God will cause us to ride in high and great places of the earth, in Jesus' name. (1 Corinthians 15: 5- 10; Genesis 38:29; Isaiah 58:14)

- In the name of Jesus, I will not be demoted, nor be stagnant. I will be the one to do the good and great assignments assigned by God for my destiny. Queen Esther replaced Queen Vashti, Judas was replaced by another disciple. I reject this evil of somebody else taking my great places in destiny, in Jesus' name (Mention as many people you want to pray this prayer over). My destiny rejects this evil. Another will not take my place in my marriage, family, church of God, and in anything God has assigned for my destiny. I will not be replaced. I will be what God has packaged me to be, I will do what He has ordered for my destiny, and my destiny will rise and shine, in Jesus' name. (Galatians 2: 11- 14, Acts 10: 14, Esther 2:4, 17, Acts 1: 16-26, Psalms 109:8)

- After the order of Pharez, who became first born by favor, breaking cultural barriers, I break through cultural barriers, governmental barriers, physical, mental, spiritual, people, and all barriers, in Jesus' name. As I step out today, I will be divinely favored and repositioned to be the number one in what I am going to do today. None will be able to hold me down or stand against me all the days of my life. I thank you Lord, for you have heard my prayers, in Jesus' name. (Genesis 38:29 -30; Joshua 1:5)

- Father, in the name of Jesus, after the order of the widow of Zarephath, who through favor, enjoyed unending provisions when the nation she lived in suffered drought, I decree and declare, no dryness in my family. After the order of the Sidon widow, whatever jar of oil represents in my life, the jar will never run dry. My life will not be dry. My home will not be dry. My ministry will not be dry. My business will not be dry, and my pockets will never run dry. I decree, no dryness or drought in all areas of my life, in Jesus' name. (1 Kings 17: 14 -16).

- By the authority in the name of Jesus, as the Shunammite woman, by favor, got 'inside information' from Prophet Elisha and escaped seven years of famine in her town, throughout this day, week, month, and year, I will escape all evils and misfortunes befalling others.

- Father, anoint my inner eyes. Anoint my mind. Give me ideas, innovations, and concepts that will lift me above the economy of my time, in Jesus' name (2 Kings 8:1).

- By favor, the king gave the Shunammite woman every benefit due her from the time she left the city, until her return, seven years after! The woman enjoyed the best of two worlds! Father, you are the same God, yesterday, today, and forever, by your instrument of favor, send helpers of destiny along my way today. Let me receive in large measures whatever I need to make my life colorful. Whatever I have lost will be restored and what is stolen, will be returned. I will enjoy God's abundant provisions everywhere I go in the world, in Jesus' name (2 Kings 8:6).

- Lord, by your instrument of favor, after the order of the widow of Sidon, as the bin of her flour was continuously replenished by your invincible hands, I decree and declare, there shall be continuous supply of everything I need. I have unending breakthroughs, uncountable blessings and unstoppable progress, in Jesus' name. This very day, my cups of favor will overflow. I will have more than enough and will be a blessing to nations, in Jesus' name (1 Kings 17:16).

- The Bible says that each day has enough trouble of its own. By the authority in the name of Jesus, as the Shunammite woman escaped drought and dryness for seven years, I decree that throughout this day, week, month, and year, I receive the anointing to escape all evils programmed for these periods, in Jesus' name. (Pray these prayers over your loved ones also) (Matthew 6:34, 2 Kings 8: 1).

- The Shunammite woman enjoyed seven years of plenty in the city she relocated to and when she returned to her own city, the king ordered that every blessing that was due her for the seven years she was not in town be given to her! In the name of Jesus, the King of kings already paid for the deliveries of all my benefits. So, I declare that every benefit due me from birth that eluded me be speedily delivered into my life, in Jesus' name. As God used His instrument of favor to restore this woman to her former high position, I receive restoration of my name, dignity, lost opportunities, lost years, and all the good things due me, in Jesus' name.

- The case of this woman was a "win-win" case. When she was away from the dry city, she won; when she came back to her town after the famine was over, she won. She was an all-round winner! I decree the "win-win" anointing upon my life, career, business, and everything I lay my hands upon. I will win wherever I turn. I will win among hostile people; I will win among friendly people; I will win in the plane, on the road, in the train, and on the sea. I will win wherever I go, in Jesus' name. I am an all-round winner, in the name of Jesus.

Prayer Declarations

- I decree all the above blessings upon your life. Favor will deliver into your life everything the favor of God can do in the world. You will be selected by favor, repositioned by favor, promoted by favor, provided for by favor, and all you have lost will be restored by the instrument of favor.

- I prophesy upon your life every evil and misfortune flowing around the city you live in will miss you and your family members. May the heavens open upon you, as the Shunammite woman enjoyed seven years of abundance she never labored for. By favor, you will enjoy harvests without labor. You shall receive blessings more than the labor of your hands. As Prophet Elisha's assistant, Gehazi, was with the king when the woman went into the palace, God will position people in market places, high places, and all places, that will speak great things about you. You will always be at the right places, at the right times, with the right people, doing the right things, and achieving right results, in Jesus' name.

- By the instrument of favor, you will never be replaced in your divinely appointed places. You will not build for another to inhabit; you will not plant for another to eat your harvests. Your hands laboring in the land of the living will not be found missing in the years of harvest. I decree, as the days of the trees, so shall be your years in the land of the living, in Jesus' name. (Psalms 84:11, Matthew 6:34, 2 Kings 8: 5-6, Isaiah 65: 22)

9
EZEKIEL: VISIONS OF GOD, WORD OF GOD AND HAND OF GOD

As we noted in the previous chapter, one of the blessings that Ezekiel enjoyed when he had his open heaven experience was that he saw visions of God. He said it himself in Ezekiel 1:3, "I saw visions of God."

Biblically, nobody can see God and live. However, when God in His graciousness shows what we call, "visions of God," it is always to show His glory, some parts of His presence, or make one to see His angels. One may also hear and see some supernatural things. God is God and He can show and manifests Himself to anyone, as He chooses. Some Prophets of old and many Christians have seen the glory of God. Sometimes, God even manifests and shows His glory to unbelievers, in order to draw them to Himself. I have also been privileged to see God's glory a few times.

It is always very exciting to see God's glory. Such visits are always very humbling experiences. Nobody is shown visions of God's glory so that they can brag or think they are higher than others. If you check the pages of the Bible, all those who saw visions of God's presence or glory were scared and many fell down as if they were dead. They were only able to receive and see properly after being strengthened by God Himself.

Purpose of God's Revelation of Glory

When God shows His glory, it can be for purification, instructions, warnings, or trainings – to show a person things that will happen in the future, and so on, depending on the type of things seen. Many times, the person who is experiencing the visions of God will know heaven's expectations of what to do. God has shown me so many visions such as the endless pit of darkness and fear unbelievers fall into as soon as they die. I have heard and seen flowers singing beautifully on the streets of heaven. I have heard the choir of heavens sing and it was very captivating.

The essence of such visitations in my own life have been for so many different reasons, but I can tell you that they were scary experiences to me. Yet, they generated continuous love of God, as well as a heart to honor and appreciate His love, faithfulness, and care over mere mortal men like us that He created.

Pray this:

- Father, as you opened Ezekiel's eyes and he saw visions from you, help me to see good things everywhere I will go today. My eyes will not see evil, my ears will hear good reports today, and my legs will take me to prepared provision.

- Lord, the Psalmist cried out to you, that you should open his eyes of understanding for him to behold wondrous things of your word. I pray after that order, in the name of Jesus, let my eyes of understanding be opened. Help me to see beyond the natural eyes. Anoint my inner eyes to see and know the deep things of your word and my world (Ezekiel 1:1; Psalms 119;18).

POTENCY OF GOD'S WORD

The next blessing of open heavens that Ezekiel enjoyed was that the Word of God came expressly to him. Ezekiel 1:3 says, "the word of the Lord came expressly to Ezekiel the priest, the son of Buzi, in the land of the Chaldeans by the River Chebar; and the hand of the Lord was upon him there."

Any Christian, living a life without the Word of God, will live below his or her maximum capacity. The person may be successful, but it will not be a huge success, compared to when the Christian makes the Word a daily meal. The Word of God is so important that even our Savior Jesus reminded us that men should not live by bread alone but by every Word coming from the mouth of God (Matthew 4:4). He is simply saying that while the food we eat daily is important to nourish and empower our body, it is not as important as the word of God that will give us abundant life.

Jesus is not saying that we should not eat, He is saying that we should eat, but physical food is not the only thing you should eat DAILY if you want to really "live" life. Your true essence of living the kind of life God has for you can only be achieved as you "eat" His Word. The daily physical food we eat is important, but its importance pales, in comparison with the importance of the word of God.

One of the consequences the Israelites suffered anytime they turned away from God, was the scarcity of God's Word or absence of words and directions from God. They lost battles whenever God didn't speak to them and were victorious when they turned to God.

David was a man after God's own heart. However, the Word of God was one major thing that contributed to his success and victories. David always consulted God before doing anything. Sadly, he did not consult God when he saw Bathsheba, and he suffered gravely for it. May the love for God and His Word continue to burn in all of us, amen.

Pray this:

- The Word of God was heard by Ezekiel expressly. From now on, no more delay of God's words and promises in my life. God's words are His plans and promises for my life. Therefore, I decree, this day, this week, this month, this year, and this season, God's promises will no longer be delayed in my life. They will come to pass speedily, in Jesus' name.

- All the promises of God are "Yes" and "Amen," they are guaranteed to be delivered and to come to pass. I decree, my heavens are opened; no more hindrances and no more delays, in Jesus' name.

- As I step out today, I receive by faith, instructions from the Holy Spirit that will make my life beautiful. As I read God's Word and hear His Word, I receive understanding of the word. I will know what to do, become what the Word promises, and I will move from glory to glory, in Jesus' name.

FULLNESS AND PRODUCTIVITY BY THE WORD

In Luke 5:5, Peter said, "Master, we have toiled all night and caught nothing; nevertheless at Your word I will let down the net." Peter stepped out, based on the word that proceeded from the Lord Jesus; and the man who had caught nothing after toiling day and night, caught many fishes.

Pray this:

- In the name of Jesus, I reject nothingness syndrome. I will not work for nothing, eat for nothing, live for nothing, or labor for nothing.

- After the order of Peter's experience, as I step out today by God's word, I will come back home with "too many blessings." My cup will run over with blessings.

- As Peter had to call his friends in the other boat and filled their boats with fishes, Father, bless me and make me a blessing to others, and to nations, in Jesus' name. (Luke 5: 6-7).

HEALING AND CLEANSING BY THE WORD

When Jesus gave a Word to the ten lepers, they were all healed. Naaman was healed of his leprosy after obeying the instruction from Elijah. By the Word of God from Paul and Silas, the crippled man by the gate called Beautiful received instant healing.

Pray this:

In Jesus' name, the Word of God is medicine to my body (Proverbs 4:20-22), therefore, I am healed, I am cleansed, and purified from all diseases. Jesus is the Word that came from heaven, and by His stripes, I am totally healed and free of all sicknesses and diseases.

Prayer Declarations

- Every Word of Jesus caused miracles in peoples' lives. Jesus said, "Go and show yourself to the priest" and ten lepers were cleansed. His instruction of "Come" to Peter made Peter to walk on water. I decree open heavens upon you. God's Words will be delivered expressly to you, daily. It will cause you to walk boldly where others are afraid. God's Word will cleanse, purify and heal you from all sicknesses of life.

- I prophesy God's Words over every area of your life. You will not struggle or toil; God will open unusual doors of opportunities for you. God will cause you to ride in the high places of life. You will dip your feet in oil and suck honey from the rocks, in Jesus' name. You are blessed!

The Awesomeness of God's Hand

Ezekiel felt the mighty hand of God, as the heavens were opened upon him. Ezekiel 1:3 says, "and the hand of the LORD was upon him there."

The hand of God is symbolic of many things, including God's sovereign power in creation and interventions in the affairs of people and events of life. To have God's hands upon the life of a Christian will definitely set the person on a higher dimension that will give him or her an enviable first class lifestyle!

Below are few verses showing what God's hands will do in your life. You can formulate prayer points for yourself and loved ones from these verses.

God's hands will perfect and establish you.

The psalmist rightly declares, "The LORD will accomplish that which concerns me; Your [unwavering] lovingkindness, O LORD, endures forever—Do not abandon the works of Your own hands" (Psalms 138:8).

God's hands will satisfy your desires and give you food.

Psalms 145:15-16 says, "The eyes of all look to You [in hopeful expectation], And You give them their food in due time. You open Your hand And satisfy the desire of every living thing."

God's hands will bring judgement upon your enemies.

God says in Zephaniah 1:4, "I will also stretch out My hand [in judgment] against Judah And against all the inhabitants of Jerusalem. And I will cut off *and* destroy the remnant of Baal from this place, And the names *and* remembrance of the idolatrous priests along with the [false] priests."

God's hands will protect you and use you locally and globally.

Isaiah 42:6 assures, "I, the LORD, have called You in righteousness, And will hold Your hand; I will keep You and give You as a covenant to the people, As a light to the Gentiles.

Some other truths about God's hands that you can formulate prayers from are:

- The hand of God does glorious and marvelous things for his children (Psalms 118:16).

- God's hands laid the foundations of the earth (Isaiah 48:13).

- By God's outstretched hands, nothing is difficult for Him (Jereniah32:17).

PRAYER DECLARATIONS

It is written in 1 Kings 18:46, " Then the hand of the Lord came upon Elijah [giving him supernatural strength]. He girded up his loins and outran Ahab to the entrance of Jezreel [nearly twenty miles]." After the above order, I decree over your life – No more delays. No matter all those who have gone ahead of you, after the order of Ezekiel, God's hands will lift you and you will make up for your lost grounds and lost years. Your promotion will be speedily delivered. Money to start that business will be speedily delivered. No more delays of your progress. As God's hands was upon Elijah, and he received supernatural strength for speedy arrival to his destination, whatever is needed for your speedy arrival to your next dimensions of fulfilment will be delivered by God's hands, in Jesus' name.

I decree blessings upon you and your loved ones. As God's hands lifted Ezekiel and he was able to see the problems of his time, as well as to hear solutions to the problems, God's hands will rest upon your family. Heavens will open permanently upon you and you will receive daily instructions for your life. God will give you solutions and ideas that will change your world, in Jesus' name, amen.

10
JESUS CHRIST: DIVINE SEAL OF APPROVAL FROM OPEN HEAVENS

Jesus Christ was the Son of God, yet He needed and got open heaven experiences. If Jesus had open heavens experiences, then you must seek to have them too. This is especially important, considering Christ's promise in John 14:12 that believers will do greater works than He did. If Jesus is expecting us to do greater works, then we should have some of the great experiences, such as open heavens, that He had.

Here's how Jesus' open heavens experience is described in Matthew 3: 13-17, "Then Jesus came from Galilee to John at the Jordan to be baptized by him. And John tried to prevent Him, saying, 'I need to be baptized by You, and are You coming to me?' But Jesus answered and said to him, 'Permit it to be so now, for thus it is fitting for us to fulfill all righteousness.' Then he allowed Him. When

He had been baptized, Jesus came up immediately from the water; and behold, the heavens were opened to Him, and He saw the Spirit of God descending like a dove and alighting upon Him. And suddenly a voice came from heaven, saying, 'This is My beloved Son, in whom I am well pleased.' "

Points to note from the above narration include:

1. The humility of Jesus through submission to John for baptism.

Jesus traveled from Galilee to meet John for baptism. Children of God should be humble to do whatever is right in righteousness for God's kingdom.

There are CEOs, bank executives and millionaires that labor as church workers in different churches, in the body of Christ.

Every child of God is saved to serve and not to sit in God's kingdom.

2. The sensitivity of John to the Spirit and to his assignment.

John's humility and sensitivity to the Spirit is worth emulating by the Christians of today. John knew that Jesus was greater than he was; he said it openly in John 1:30 that he was not even worthy to fix the lace of Jesus' sandals, wow! One of the reasons some Christians have closed heavens and stagnancy is due to pride. Like John, Christians should learn to be in the spirit to celebrate God's grace on others and not be bashful in appreciating them publicly. Refuse to join those who spread damaging and derogatory news about others because God is blessing them or is using them in a higher capacity than you.

3. Christians should walk in humility and sensitivity to the Spirit of God.

Any Christian who desires open heavens must walk in humility and sensitivity to the Spirit of God. Learn to be quiet and not be part of those destroying God's church or God's children. God needs all of us and we should build His Kingdom and not tear ourselves apart.

4. Christians should be sensitive enough to know when to move forward.

Although John was humble and he tried to stop Jesus from being baptized, Christians should be sensitive to know when to move forward or back off in the matters of other peoples' lives and their own lives. If Abraham had not been sensitive in the spirit, he would have killed Isaac. He [Abraham] could have insisted that God said to sacrifice his only son. If John had not been sensitive to God's Spirit, He could have hindered the baptism of Jesus. Even the donkey of Balaam knew to stop and not move at the presence of the angel of God.

Pray this:

- My father and my God, anoint my eyes and ears. Help me to be sensitive to your voice. Help me to know when to say "No" and when to say "Yes." Teach me also how to say "Yes" and "No." Help me to be sensitive to your Holy Spirit.

- In Jesus' name, I will not try to force open the doors God Himself has shut, and I will not shut doors that God has opened. I will not be a hinderer to God's move in my life and the lives of others. I will cooperate with God to accomplish His plans for my life, in Jesus' name. (Revelation 3:7, Ezekiel 11: 19 -20).

HUMILITY AS KEY TO OPEN HEAVENS

Jesus' humility throughout His ministry on earth still humbles me. His humility began from His birth to His ascension to heaven. There were many occasions during His stay on earth that He should have used His power and anointing to circumvent, cancel, destroy, address, or prevent some of the difficult situations He found Himself in. In Matthew 26:53, Jesus told those who rushed to arrest Him, "Or do you think that I cannot now pray to My Father, and He will provide Me with more than twelve legions of angels?"

Wow, Jesus could have destroyed those who wanted to kill Him, but He controlled Himself. One necessary virtue for all Christians to emulate in life is to gain mastery over the flesh. Self-mastery is the soil that germinates and produces humility. Someone has defined humility as, "Strength under control." Let us, as today's Christians follow the examples of our Savior, Jesus Christ. Many Christians want promotion, progress, and prosperity. The Bible has given us the formula for achieving this and more. The Holy Spirit will help bring God's promises to fruition in your life, as you humble yourself and connect to Him.

Pray this (based on Matthew 3: 12 -17):

- Jesus came out of the river immediately and there were good results. As Jesus came out of water and immediately the heavens opened upon Him, I pray and decree that as I step out today, I will enjoy the grace of "Immediate results." I decree there will be no delay and no holding back of my blessings. There shall be speedy delivery of my blessings and speedy accomplishments of my plans, in Jesus' name. Nothing good that I want, need, or desire today will be withheld from me, in Jesus' name (Habakkuk 2:3, Ezekiel 12:22).

- The heavens opened upon Jesus. After the order of Jesus' open heavens, my own heavens will open, as I do everything I need to do today. Heavens will open upon me and everything I touch will prosper, and all the benefits and blessings of open heavens will be enjoyed by me today, in Jesus' name. (Psalms 1:3,

Deuteronomy 28:12).

- As I step out again on this day, heavens will not be closed upon my person, upon my destiny and the works of my hands, in Jesus' name. I will be met with God's favor everywhere I go and things will not be difficult for me. My heavens will not turn to bronze and my prayers will not be blocked. I will return to my destination in wellness and success. No destruction and no bad news, in Jesus' name (Haggai 1:10 -11; Deuteronomy 28: 23 -24).

- John saw the Spirit descending as a dove and a lighting upon Jesus. After the order of Jesus' experience on that day, as I step out into my world today (business, classrooms, career, etc.), Father, let your signature and stamp of approval be seen upon me life. As John saw your Spirit upon Jesus, demarcate and showcase my life and everything I do with the glory of your presence. Let people see your mark of distinction and excellence upon my life, in Jesus' name.

- As John acknowledged God's presence upon Jesus, as Laban acknowledged God's presence upon Jacob, and as Potiphar acknowledged your presence upon Joseph, I decree that everyone that sees me today will acknowledge and validate your presence upon me, in Jesus' name. (John 1: 32 -34, Genesis 30:27, Genesis 30:2,5).

- I decree that God's glory will rest upon my life today. I decree that as many people that I will come in contact with today will affirm and confirm God's glory in my life, in Jesus' name. As John saw the Holy Spirit descend as a dove upon Jesus, I decree by the authority in the name of Jesus, that the Holy Spirit will envelope me, guide me, help me, affirm, and confirm me. Good and great things will be seen by everyone in my life today, in Jesus' name (John 1:32; John 14:25)

- Father, in the name of Jesus, open people's eyes of understanding and let them honor me with the honor of your presence. None will look down on my person and none will withhold from me the benefits and favor you have apportioned for me today, in Jesus' name (Proverbs 3:28; Luke 24:31).

Conquering Barricades

It is possible to face difficulties and challenges from the same people God has packaged to favor and bless you. Instead of being favored by people, someone can be frustrated and hurt by people. This sometimes happens because Satan can interrupt peoples' lives and block, delay, or divert good things to flow from one person to the other. People that should honor and help others will see or hear lies and negativities about them. Thus, instead of helping them, they will withhold help from them or may even hurt them!

Pray this:

- I declare upon my life, every mark of failure, mark of evil, mark of hatred, mark of lies, and all negative marks that is preventing people from helping me are removed by fire right now, in Jesus' name.

- I decree that immediate and positive results will be following me. I decree from this moment, all evil marks of negativities are replaced by marks of favor and honor, in Jesus' name (Genesis 4:15, Psalms 105: 14-15).

POWER OF DIVINE AFFIRMATION AND CONFIRMATION

Matthew 3:17 says, "behold, a voice from heaven said, 'This is My beloved Son, in whom I am well-pleased *and* delighted!'"

The voice of God the Father was heard from heaven and God affirmed and confirmed the Person of Christ and the pleasure He gave God the Father. Affirmation and confirmation brings out the authenticity of a person's character and purpose. When a governmental official or someone in a high position affirms or confirms, let's say for example, an entrepreneur or a trader, such a person will become a huge success in the town where such affirmation and confirmation has taken place. The confirmation and affirmation means the higher authority is vouching, putting the stamp of approval, and asking everyone to do business with the person that is so confirmed and affirmed.

Confirmation and affirmation is a paid advertisement of the person by the higher ranked person. The popularity and success of the person being confirmed is dependent upon the rank or position of the higher person. If the president or king of the town does the confirmation and affirmation, the person will become a celebrity overnight! Can you now imagine if the person affirming and confirming you is higher than the highest person in your country, and He is higher than the highest person in the world!

The person advertising you is the owner and creator of the world, and everybody and everything is subject to Him! Imagine if God speaks loud in an audible voice and confirms your person, your purpose, and His plans in the presence of a huge crowd, wow – your destiny will radiate God's glory forever!

This is what happens when the heavens are opened upon you. This is the reason you must take and pray the following prayer points seriously. Pray them for yourself daily and slot in the names of your loved ones, your business and everything you lay your hands upon.

Pray this:

- My Father, as I step out today and I go about my activities, let your presence affirm and confirm me. As there was a mark of distinction upon the Israelites' in

Goshen, affirm, confirm, and put a mark of distinction upon my person, my purpose, Your presence upon my life, Your plans for my life, and Your power at work in my life. Affirm and confirm my health, the work of my hands, my family, and my ministry, in the name of Jesus. (Exodus 33: 12 -16, Exodus 8:22).

- Oh God, my heavenly Father, through Your affirmation and confirmation, remove and take away toiling, struggling, and difficulties from my life, in the name of Jesus. By Your open heavens, assault and insult everything and everyone trying to subdue, suppress, submerge, and subtract from my destiny, in the name of Jesus.

- Oh Lord my God, by the instrument of Your open heavens, release fresh grace, fresh fire of the Holy Ghost to fall upon my household, and everything I lay my hands upon, this day, this week, this month, and this season of my life. Let your open heavens speak loud and clear upon me. Release higher grace and greater anointing to affirm and confirm everything that I stand for, in Jesus' name. (Matthew 3:11, Proverbs 4:18).

The affirmation and confirmation of God upon a person will definitely advertise the person to all the necessary and appropriate places globally. 1 Corinthian 10:26 says, "for the earth is the Lord's, and all its fullness." It is important that Christians should appreciate the grace given by God to spend time in His presence. By honoring this important invitation, a believer can have the heavens opened continually and enjoy unlimited blessings of open heavens. Jesus enjoyed global advertisement of His ministry, through the open heavens experienced by Him!

GLOBAL ADVERTISEMENT THROUGH OPEN HEAVENS

Luke 4:37, "Immediately the news about Him spread everywhere throughout the district surrounding Galilee."

Luke 5:15, "But the news about Him was spreading farther, and large crowds kept gathering to hear Him and to be healed of their illnesses."

Based on the above scriptures, the fame of Jesus went abroad, all over the nations, without:

- Facebook
- Internet
- Instagram
- Twitter
- We chat
- WhatsApp
- Telephone
- Television
- Radio and all the social media platforms of today.

My friend, open heavens can divinely advertise your destiny more than all these social media accounts combined!

Pray this:

- Oh Lord God of open heavens, open Your heavens upon my destiny, my career, and the work of my hands. After the order of Jesus' destiny, that His fame went abroad, make my business, my work, and ministry become a global phenomenon, to the glory of Your name. Advertise what I stand for and what I carry, in Jesus' name. (Luke 5: 15, Proverbs 4:18).

BLESSED BY BAPTISM

Matthew 3:16-17 says, " After Jesus was baptized, He came up immediately out of the water; and behold, the heavens were opened, and he (John) saw the Spirit of God descending as a dove and lighting on Him (Jesus), and behold, a voice from heaven said, 'This is My beloved Son, in whom I am well-pleased *and* delighted!' "

Six major things happened to Jesus after He was baptized:

- His heavens opened.
- John saw the Spirit of God upon Him.
- The Spirit alighted upon Him.
- The voice of God was heard from heaven.
- The voice confirmed and affirmed Jesus' identity.

- The voice confirmed the pleasure and delight of the Father upon the Son.

I pray that the six blessings above will rest upon you, too, in Jesus' name.

Prayer Declarations

- In Jesus' name, I decree open heavens upon your life. As the heavens opened upon Jesus, out of all those who went for water baptism, may God's single you out for uncommon favor and undeniable promotion.

- In Matthew 3:17, the Bible says God spoke openly that Jesus pleased Him! I pray that God will be pleased and delighted with you today. Your thoughts, actions, and reactions will receive affirmation from God, in Jesus' name. Everywhere you and your family members will go today, everyone will favor you and will be pleased and delighted in you, in Jesus' name.

It is very pertinent for you to pray daily that whatever good you do will not be covered. You should also pray this important prayer for your loved ones.

11

SUNDRY WONDERS FROM OPEN HEAVENS

This chapter contains different scriptures showing some people of covenant with God and their open heavens experiences.

JACOB'S LADDER EXPERIENCE

Genesis 28: 10-15 reads, "Now Jacob went out from Beersheba and went toward Haran. So he came to a certain place and stayed there all night, because the sun had set. And he took one of the stones of that place and put it at his head, and he lay down in that place to sleep. Then he dreamed, and behold, a ladder was set up on the earth, and its top reached to heaven; and there the angels of God were ascending and descending on it. And behold, the Lord stood above it and said: 'I am the Lord God of Abraham your father and the God of Isaac; the land on which you lie I will give to you and your descendants. Also your descendants shall be as the dust of the earth; you shall spread abroad to the west and the east, to the north and the south; and in you and in your seed all the families of the earth shall be blessed. Behold, I am with you and will keep[c] you wherever you go, and will bring you back to this land; for I will not leave you until I have done what I have spoken to you.' "

Pray this:

- Wherever I go today, heavens will open over me.

- As there were angels ascending and descending upon Jacob, I pray that there will be increased angelic activities upon me. They will protect me, provide for me, make ways for me, and fight for me, in Jesus' name.

- Angels will ascend with my requests and descend with answers to my prayers.

- God's presence will go with me to all the places I am going today, in Jesus' name.

- In Jesus' name, after the order of verse 15, the Lord is with me, He will keep me wherever I go today. He will bring me back safely, and He will fulfill all His plans over me today.

- Father, give me divine instructions for this very day, instructions for my lifting and progress, in Jesus' name.

- Jacob had nothing before crossing the Jordan; he used a rock as a pillow and had only one staff. But on his return journey, he said in Genesis 32:10, "With only my staff [long ago] I crossed over this Jordan, and now I have become [blessed and increased into these] two groups [of people]." Father, I decree and declare that this will become my testimony. I will return today, from this trip, this journey, and will come back, blessed, prosperous, and victorious, in Jesus' name.

MANOAH'S ANGELIC VISIT REQUEST

Judges 13:8-11 says, "Then Manoah prayed to the LORD, and said, 'O my Lord, please let the Man of God whom You sent come to us again and teach us what we shall do for the child who will be born." And God listened to the voice of Manoah, and the Angel of God came to the woman again as she was sitting in the field; but Manoah her husband *was* not with her. Then the woman ran in haste and told her husband, and said to him, "Look, the Man who came to me the *other* day has just now appeared to me!' So Manoah arose and followed his wife. When he came to the Man, he said to Him, 'Are You the Man who spoke to this woman?' And He said, '*I am.*' "

Pray this:
- Manoah was not present both times the angels visited his wife. My father and my God, as your heavens will open over different places and people today, help me to be a partaker in Jesus' name.

- As I step out today, I will not miss my divine moments and angelic visitations that will lead to the coronation of my work, career, business, and destiny.

- Father, I receive heavenly and angelic visitations that will cancel years of suffering, dryness, bareness, and unproductiveness, in Jesus' name.

- As Manoah prayed for a re-visitation and God heard him, I decree open heavens over my life and destiny.

- I decree re-visitations of lost opportunities. God will rewind the good opportunities and bring back good relationships. Good benefits that eluded me in the past will suddenly be released now, in Jesus' name.

STEPHEN'S VISION OF THE STANDING CHRIST

Acts 7: 55-56 reads, "But he, full of the Holy Spirit, gazed into heaven and saw the glory of God, and Jesus standing at the right hand of God. And he said, "Behold, I see the heavens opened, and the Son of Man standing at the right hand of God."

Prayer this:

- Stephen was chosen among others because he was full of faith and led by the Holy Spirit. Father, in the name of Jesus, by your open heavens, let me be preferred, selected and appointed to positions of honor today (Acts 6:5).

- As your heavens open upon my life, fill me with the fullness of your Holy Spirit. I will be led and directed by your Holy Spirit.

- I receive the fullness of your Holy Spirit that will give me full help to see what I need to see, full knowledge to know what I need to know, full strength to do what I need to do today, so I can achieve fullness of success, in Jesus' name.

- As Stephen saw the heavens opened and He saw the glory of God, I decree in Jesus' name, my heavens are opened. I will see good things today, hear beautiful news today, and meet helpers of destiny that will facilitate events for the beautification of my destiny, in Jesus' name.

Prayer Declarations

- As you step out to do your work, go for the interview, sit for the examination, travel to places, go to the hospital, and as you go around on this day to do the things in your heart, God's glory will rest upon you. The Holy Spirit will help you, protect you, and guide you. May God anoint your eyes of understanding, as Stephen saw the heavens opened. You will see what you need to see, know what you need to know. None will stand against you, all will favor you and cooperate with you throughout today, in Jesus' name.

- As you are home, cooking, cleaning, sleeping, and

doing whatever you do at home, you will be full of the Holy Spirit. You will operate in fullness and you will not run on "low" or operate in scantiness. The grace of "fullness" is upon you. Your cups of joy will be full, your head will be full of oil, and your pockets will not be empty but will be full of money. You are full of wisdom, knowledge, and understanding. Wherever you go today and whatever you have planned to do will turn out positively, in Jesus' name.

- The Bible says in Colossians 3:1 that Christ is seated at the right of God. However, Stephen saw Jesus, standing at the right of God. Jesus was probably moved by the fullness of faith and fullness of the Holy Spirit of Stephen. In Mark 10:49a, Jesus also stopped when He heard blind Bartimaeus's voice. I decree and declare that due to heavens opening upon your life, people in high places and all places will stand in your favor. If they are sleeping, sitting, or engaged, God will move them to stop and stand to help you. Your voice will command honor and attention, and everything created, seen and unseen, the sun, the moon, stars, and galaxies will help to coordinate, facilitate, and coronate your destiny today, in Jesus' name.

JESUS' OTHER OPEN HEAVENS EXPERIENCE

Matthew 17: 1-6 reveals, "Six days later Jesus took with Him Peter and James and John the brother of James, and led them up on a high mountain by themselves. And His appearance changed dramatically in their presence; and His face shone [with heavenly glory, clear and bright] like the sun, and His clothing became as white as light. And behold, Moses and Elijah appeared to them, talking with Jesus. Then Peter began to speak and said to Jesus, 'Lord, it is good *and* delightful *and* auspicious that we are here; if You wish, I will put up three [sacred] tents here—one for You, one for Moses, and one for Elijah.' While he was still speaking, behold, a bright cloud overshadowed them, and a voice from the cloud said, 'This is My beloved Son, with whom I am well-pleased *and* delighted! Listen to Him!' When the disciples heard it, they fell on their faces and were terrified."

Pray this:

- Lord, as the heavens opened upon Jesus, let your heavens open upon my health, marriage, children, business, family, ministry, education, and let your glory appear upon all these areas, in Jesus' name.

- Father, by your open heavens, as the appearance of Jesus changed, change everything that needs to be changed in my life – my character, my emotions, my destiny, and my finances.

- Lord, as the face of Jesus shone with heavenly glory, wherever I go to on this very day, envelope me with the glory of your presence that will make me to be received, respected and honored, in Jesus' name.

- Father, as you audibly affirmed Jesus' authority and legitimacy, wherever I go today, affirm your presence, power, and plans over my life, in Jesus' name.

APOSTLE JOHN'S INVITATION TO THE END TIMES

Revelations 4:1 says, "After this I looked, and behold, a door standing open in heaven! And the first voice which I had heard, like *the sound* of a [war] trumpet speaking with me, said, 'Come up here, and I will show you what must take place after these things.' "

John was privileged to be selected out of those who followed Jesus to see the mysteries shown in the book of Revelations.

John was the bridge between his time and the end of time. He was the disciple who did not die, and he saw the end of the earth and the new heavens (Matthew 16:28).

Pray this:

- Father, in the name of Jesus, as the heavens opened upon John and he moved higher and saw things yet to come, let my eyes of understanding open to the things of the Spirit. Show me the things that will make for my peace, promotion, and wellness, in life, in Jesus' name (Luke 19: 42).

- Father, you selected John out of the disciples and showed him the future. You selected the sons of Issachar out of the Israelites, to have understanding of the times and the knowledge of what to do (1 Chronicles 12:32). Father, by your favor, select me to be the bridge between my generation and the future. I receive wisdom to have the understanding of the times and the knowledge of what the Church should do. I thank you for this, in Jesus' name.

12

UNLOCKING THE HEAVENS ABOVE YOU

While it is the prerogative of God to open or close His heavens, there are things you can do to open or close the heavens over your life. There are things you can do to open your heavens, especially if loving God and advancing His kingdom is a major priority in your heart.

Just as Sister Frustration (who later became Felicitation) in the first chapter of this book, any believer can break the yokes of frustration, afflictions, failures, and hopelessness to enjoy a life of permanent open heavens. Also, any Christian who wants to advance in their Christian walk, who wants to know God deeper, and anyone who desires intimacy with God, can engage in kingdom practices that will be discussed in this chapter.

The good news is that whoever has a living relationship with God does not have to live under closed heavens.

Jesus has already paid the price to make your life colorful, beautiful, and fruitful. Sometimes, as Christians, we are aware of the price Jesus paid on our behalf, but our prayers are amiss and we still wallow in dryness, drought, and evil family patterns.

However, by engaging in the kingdom practices discussed in this chapter, your Christian walk will be enhanced, you will be empowered, and your life cannot stay the same. No matter what has plagued your life so far, no matter how long the enemy has prevailed, the God of open heavens will burst His heavens on your behalf and prove Himself strong and powerful.

POWER OF APPLIED TRUTH

Some of the kingdom activities you will read below may be familiar to you. Still, I urge you to read with open mind. This is because the anointing of God upon this book will make these activities your habitual daily living. It is the application of the truth that you know and practice that will set you free. Anybody can have information on how to fly a plane. You may know all there is to know (the knowledge and the truth) about flying, but it is flying the plane without crashing that will show your knowledge about flying.

Mostly everybody addicted to smoking or drinking knows that the consequences of their habits can be disastrous. Many know the truth about the drugs, but knowing something is different from practicing it. It is when the truth you know is applied to your life and it becomes a habitual lifestyle, then, it can be said that you are free indeed.

In John 8: 32, Jesus says, "And you will know the truth, and the truth will set you free."

If you read the entire chapter of John 8, you will find that the Jews that Jesus was addressing in this context knew very well that their forefathers were slaves in Egypt; yet they were in denial. They knew the truth, but the truth did not profit them, so they remained in bondage. It is the truth you know and act upon that sets you free.

The kingdom activities listed below are eternal truths, and if they become your daily habits, you will enjoy a permanent lifestyle of open heavens. My point is, after reading this book in its entirety, grace of God to make the activities discussed in this chapter a lifestyle will fall upon you, and you can live daily under a permanent open heaven, in Jesus' name.

The Keys for Unlocking

1. Salvation

John 3:16-17, says "For God so [greatly] loved *and* dearly prized the world, that He [even] gave His [One and] only begotten Son, so that whoever believes *and* trusts in Him [as

Savior] shall not perish, but have eternal life. For God did not send the Son into the world to judge *and* condemn the world [that is, to initiate the final judgment of the world], but that the world might be saved through Him."

To enjoy a life of open heavens, you need to accept God as your Father and join His family. There are two options of fathers – God and Satan (2 Corinthians 6: 17-18; John 8:44). Connect with the right Father, God, the God of open heavens, who has the power to open His heavens over your life.

Salvation is the deliverance from sin and its consequences through the acceptance of Jesus as your Lord and Savior. Salvation is the priceless gift of God offered to mankind for the saving of their souls. All human beings descended from Adam. Unfortunately, due to the disobedience of Adam, everyone connected to him inherited the sin nature (Adamic nature of disobedience) and are doomed to spend eternity without God, in hell. (Romans 3:23, 5:12, 14). God, being a gracious God could not leave us helpless, hopeless, and eternally separated from Him. He therefore sent His only begotten Son, Jesus Christ, as the "Last Adam" (1 Corinthians 15: 45- 49).

Whoever reconnects to this Last Adam will be reconnected back to God and will spend eternal life with Him. (Romans 5:18 -19). To be saved means to be delivered and be free from the eternal judgement and punishment already prepared for those who will not accept Christ's gift of salvation. To escape and be free from this judgement, you need someone to set you free. That Someone is Jesus. He already paid the price needed by dying on the cross for the world. This qualifies Him as the only Savior of mankind (John 14:6, Acts 4:12).

How can you be saved? Salvation is free, but it is by faith (Ephesians 2:8). The steps to receive it are:

- Accept that you are lost without God. (Romans 3:23)
- You need to repent and turn back to God by asking for forgiveness of your sins. (Acts 3:19)
- Believe in your heart that Jesus came and died on the cross to save you from the penalty of sin. (Romans 6:23)
- Verbally invite Jesus to come into your life. (Revelation 3:20, Romans 10: 9-10, 13).

Once a person takes the steps above and means it in the heart, that person is translated from the family of Satan to the family of God. The person needs only to find a good church, where he or she is constantly fed with the right word of God.

2. Walking in obedience to God

Once a person is saved, you need to live a life of obeying the "Father of the house." Obedience to God is simply doing what the Father asks you to do. As you obey God, there are blessings attached to it; those blessings will follow you. One of such blessings is that the heavens will open over you (Deuteronomy 28:12). You will know what the father wants you to do from the Word of God – the Bible. You cannot pick and choose what you want to obey; otherwise, that kind of obedience is obedience to self as convenient to you. Full obedience that can profit any believer is to do whatever God wants you to do, whether it is easy or difficult, convenient or not convenient.

Jesus says in John 14:15, "You are my friends if you do what I tell you to do." Obedience to God is easy, if you depend on the Holy Spirit, who is mentioned also in this chapter. As you obey God, He will give you whatever you ask for in Jesus' name. Jesus says in John 14:14,15, "If you ask Me anything in My name [as My representative], I will do it. If you [really] love Me, you will keep *and* obey My commandments."

Blessings attached to obedience are guaranteed to those who walk in habitual obedience to God. Deuteronomy 28:1-2 reveals, "Now it shall be, if you diligently listen to *and* obey the voice of the LORD your God, being careful to do all of His commandments which I am commanding you today, the LORD your God will set you high above all the nations of the earth. All these blessings will come upon you and overtake you if you pay attention to the voice of the LORD your God."

Obey God, ask anything by faith in Jesus name, and God will fulfill His promises over you.

3. Studying the word of God daily

Jesus is the Word of God. He is the Key to your open heavens. The Word of God has unlimited blessings and one of them is the blessing of open heavens.

2 Timothy 3:16-17 says, "All Scripture is God-breathed [given by divine inspiration] and is profitable for instruction, for conviction [of sin], for correction [of error and restoration to obedience], for training in righteousness [learning to live in conformity to God's will, both publicly and privately—behaving honorably with personal integrity and moral courage]; so that the man of God may be complete *and* proficient, outfitted *and* thoroughly equipped for every good work."

The word of God brings many good things to believers. When you depend on the Holy Spirit to help you study and understand the Bible, it becomes very enjoyable to study it. If you truly want to know God intimately, you can know Him very well through His word. God is the "Word of God", every time you create time to study the Bible, you are spending time not with a book, but because God is the word, you are actually spending time with God. (John 1:1,14). As written above, the Word of God is God and the Word is likened to many things in the Bible that can profit a believer. For you to know the word is so important and should be studied daily, here are a few things the word is likened to and can do for you:

- *God* – John 1:1
- *Hammer* – As a hammer can break the hardest of rocks, the word can break us and all bad habits that can close someone's heavens (Jeremiah 23:29).
- *Fire* – The word is powerful to burn off things that are not of God (Jeremiah 23:29).
- *Mirror* – The word is likened to a mirror. As a mirror shows you how you look, the word shows you your true self (James 1: 25). This will help you to know what to change in your character.
- *Living and powerful* – The word has power to recreate your world and open your heavens (Hebrews 12:4).
- *Light* – The word will show you the paths to walk (Psalms 119:105).
- *Lamp* – The word will guide your steps right and you will not walk in darkness (Psalms 119:105).
- *Double edged sword* – The word has power to show you problems and also give you solutions to the problems revealed (Hebrews 12:4).
- *Sweet* – gives you joy (Psalms 119:103).
- *Profitable* – change your life by correcting you, instructing, train, and build your character.
- *Purify* – The word will cleanse you and make you pure from dirty thoughts (Psalms 119:9).

- *Saves* – The word can save the soul (James 1:21).

- *Food* – The word has nourishment to give life (Matthew 4:4).

There are so many benefits in the Word because the Word is God, and the benefits in God are unlimited. This is one of the reasons Satan does not want you to study the word, nor obey it. Pray that the Holy Spirit helps you daily to study and understand the word. There are many Bible apps that you can subscribe to daily that will help you in this journey.

As you study the word daily, the Word will open the heavens above you. He says in John 15:7, "If you abide in Me, and My words abide in you, you will ask what you desire, and it shall be done for you."

4. Loving God intimately

Loving God will open your heavens. The word love is an action word, which means, it makes a lover shows the love through actions, reactions, and works. Loving God is not a confession of the mouth, but an act of the will that stems from the heart, translates into the whole body and then manifests in outward obedience. Jesus defines our love for Him in John 14:15,23, "If you [really] love Me, you will keep *and* obey My commandments…Jesus answered, 'If anyone [really] loves Me, he will keep My word (teaching); and My Father will love him, and We will come to him and make Our dwelling place with him.'"

It will be easy for your heavens to be opened daily, if you are habitually loving the Father; He lives in you and will easily open His heavens over you.

Jesus has equated loving Him to obedience. Your love will be seen in what you do – love is known by what love does.

When you spend time with a person, you get to know them and fall in love with them the more.

5. Humility

Being humble will help in opening your heavens. As already hinted, Jesus, through humility, enjoyed open heavens in many ways:

- Heavens opened to announce His birth - Luke 2: 13-14
- Heavens opened when He ascended back to heaven – Acts 1: 9-12
- Heavens opened upon Him when he was baptized – Luke 3: 21-22
- Heavens opened upon Him on the mount of transfiguration – Matthew 17:1-6

Humility is a major key to progress and to get the heavens open constantly. Humility is defined in many ways, but I just simply see it as a state of submitting to the plans and purpose of God, irrespective of one's title and the cost of the submission. Humility is knowing your worth and value, but subjecting yourself to a lower standard in order to achieve a purpose.

Jesus humbled Himself throughout His existence on earth – from being born in a lowly manger to being crucified on a tree like a common thief! Jesus was God, but He did not reckon Himself as God, but yielded Himself to all the insults and shame, for the purpose of saving man. It was humility that would make Jesus go to John for baptism. This was the reason John objected to Jesus coming to him – the lower person should go to the higher, not higher to lower (Matthew 3:13-15). John should have been the one to go to Jesus, not vice versa, but because Jesus loved the Father, He yielded to everything He needed to do, in order to carry out the Father's assignment successfully. The Bible says believers of today should allow the Jesus' kind of humility to be our lifestyle – Philippians 2:5-7. Be humble and you will enjoy a bliss of open heavens!

6. Prayer

Prayer is a major key that can open a believer's heavens. Prayer takes you to God's presence – God's presence is open heavens! Prayer is the open check Jesus gave to believers to obtain anything we want from God – John 14:13-14; Matthew 7:7.

Many people also went to be baptized during the time of Jesus' baptism. However, Jesus was the only one whose heavens were opened because He prayed.

Jesus went to John in order to be baptized. Out of those who went for water baptism, John testified that he saw the heavens opened upon Jesus.

This can be seen in Luke 3: 21-22, "When all the people were baptized, it came to pass that Jesus also was baptized; and **while He prayed**, the heaven was opened. And the Holy Spirit descended in bodily form like a dove upon Him, and a voice came from heaven which said, 'You are My Beloved Son; in You I am well pleased.' "

According to the above scripture, while Jesus prayed, the heaven was opened. Since Jesus gave all believers the rights to ask for anything, everybody can pray and ask God for open heavens and God will answer the prayers.

7. Kingdom advancement projects

Kingdom advancements projects are projects or activities that can enlarge or advance God's kingdom agenda on earth. They are activities believers can practically engage in to:

- Show their love and obedience to God
- To show their love to other people
- Advance God's kingdom
- To be about God's business

Such kingdom advancements include soul winning, giving to further God's work, giving to the poor, giving to spiritual authorities, and engaging in any service that will build and not tear down God's work. Christianity is not a religion but a relationship. In every relationship, there are expectations to be met in order to have a fair and well balanced relationship. Believers have many expectations from God; this is rightly so, because He is our Father. However, God also wants us as His children to carry out certain assignments for Him in our local churches, in our families, on our jobs, and in the world at large!

One of God's expectation is for every believer to bring those who don't have a relationship with Him already. If you have been found by God, He expects you to go and find others. We are to fish out people and bring them to God. Found people, find people. Jesus came to save the lost and he has given us the same assignment – 2 Corinthians 5: 17-19. Also, in the book of John 14:16, He says, " You did not choose Me, but I chose you and appointed you that you should go and bear fruit, and *that* your fruit should remain, that whatever you ask the Father in My name, He may give you."

The fruit in this scripture is talking about souls of other people. As you win souls to God, and they remain, whatever you ask God in Jesus name, He will give to you. Get busy, talk about Jesus to the unsaved, then ask God to give you open heavens lifestyle.

8. Faith

Faith is a major key that can unlock your heavens. There are many definitions of faith. I just want to simply say that faith is believing in the existence of God, and the infallibility of His Word and promises. It is believing that God is who He says He is, He has all He says He has, and that He can do all He says He can do. Faith is believing in God, His plans, His purposes, and His word.

The believers who walk with God are all about faith.

- Believers are saved by grace through faith – Ephesians 2:8
- Believers walk by faith – 2 Corinthians 5:7
- Believers are justified by faith – Romans 3:28; Romans 5:1
- Believers live in the flesh by faith – Galatians 2:20, Hebrews 10:38
- Believers please God by faith – Hebrews 11:6
- All things are possible through faith – Mark 9; 23

Everything about a believer's walk, victories, life, and death is all about faith. If you pray for God to open the heavens above you and you believe by faith that God can do it, He will do it!

9. Speaking the language of the kingdom

The language of the kingdom is another way to get the

heavens over you to be opened. What is the language of the kingdom? When you speak positively over your life, the day, the year, and over everything, this is what I call "speaking the language of the kingdom." Joel 2:10 says, "…Let the weak say, "I am strong!"

The language of the world is, "Say it the way you see it." So, the weak will say, "I am weak." The language of the kingdom is, "Say the positive things you want, not the negative things you see." So, the weak will not say, "I am weak," but will say, "I am strong."

The words we speak have creative power embedded in them, what you speak will create the world you live in! You must not speak the negative things you see, speak what you want to see.

When God formed the world, He did not call for architects, engineers, and builders; He simply spoke what He wanted! The Bible says in Hebrews 11:3 (MSG), "By faith, we see the world called into existence by God's word, what we see created by what we don't see." Call your open heavens into existence, speak and pray the open heavens prayers in this book daily. Speak open heavens by faith, over your days, months, years, and over your daily events and you will begin to enjoy open heavens in all your ways.

Your speaking however does not begin from your mouth; it must start from your heart. You must desire to have open heavens in your heart; believe by faith that God will give you open heavens, begin to speak daily what you have believed in your heart; then you will begin to see what you are speaking - Mark 11: 22- 23!

10. Instrument of favor

We thank God for the things we can embark upon daily that will open up our heavens. There is however the key of "favor." This is not dependent on how well you can pray or what you can do. Favor is released by God upon whoever He wants. Favor is the gift given by God that transcends a person's ability, capability, or qualifications. Noah found favor with God and the open heavens that brought water of destruction to the people of his time, but lifted him and his family. Mary was not the only virgin during her time; yet the heavens opened over her, and the angel of God visited her to announce her role in humanity! God can favor you and your family by opening His heavens upon you and releasing blessings that you cannot count.

However, while favor is the prerogative of God, I believe it can be initiated by any believer. I believe anyone can move the hand of God to release favor through prayer, holy living, giving of offerings, and engaging in kingdom advancement projects (John 14:14, Genesis 6:9, and acts 10:31).

11. Tithing

Tithing is another key by which a believer can have the heavens opened. The blessings that can be derived from the diligent, constant giving of tithes are unlimited and unquantifiable. Through the obedience of giving of tithes, a believer can have open heavens, be favored, healed, promoted, become a delight, enjoy open doors, have supernatural cancellation of debts, receive answers to long awaited prayers, and have God Himself rebuke devourers in your life. The bible says in Malachi 3: 8-10, " 'Bring all the tithes (the tenth) into the storehouse, so that there may be food in My house, and test Me now in this,' says the LORD of hosts, 'if I will not open for you the windows of heaven and pour out for you [so great] a blessing until there is no more room to receive it. Then I will rebuke the devourer (insects, plague) for your sake and he will not destroy the fruits of the ground, nor will your vine in the field drop *its grapes* [before harvest],' says the LORD of hosts. 'All nations shall call you happy *and* blessed, for you shall be a land of delight," says the LORD of hosts.' "

12. Holy Spirit operations

The Holy Spirit is the third person of the Godhead, currently on earth, living in every believer so that believers will not be helpless, hopeless, or useless. John 14: 26 says, "But the Helper (Comforter, Advocate, Intercessor—Counselor, Strengthener, Standby), the Holy Spirit, whom the Father will send in My name [in My place, to represent Me and act on My behalf], He will teach you all things" [Amplified].

The Holy Spirit is a sevenfold, perfect Help for believers. He is in us and will help us like He helped Jesus. The Holy Spirit wants to help us do greater works than Jesus did. As a believer, the Holy Spirit can help in opening the heavens above you as you engage Him daily. As you speak in your heavenly language, He will help bring your heart desires and the plans of God to fruition in your life. (Romans 8:28, Jude 1:20).

Other means by which the heavens can be opened are:

- Walking in love
- Walking in forgiveness
- Walk in obedience to God
- Charitable work of giving to the poor, widows, orphans.
- Singing songs of praises
- Worshipping and ministering to God

PRAYER DECLARATIONS

As you have read this book on open heavens, I pray for a permanent opening of God's heavens upon you. All these blessings will come upon you and overtake you:

- Heavens will open upon you.

- You will be preferred above your peers and selected for favor.

- God will pour showers of blessings upon you.

- The latter rain and former rain will converge upon you for unlimited blessings.

- God will do you good, better than ever.

- God's hands will rest strongly upon your life.

- God's hands will lift you above those who have gone ahead of you in your career.

- God's hands will move the hands of people to supply everything you need for every stage of life, in Jesus' name.

- God will cause you to ride in the high places of life.
- You will not peck floors like chicken, God will fly you and showcase you as an eagle.
- You will not eat crumbs, but you will eat the best of the land you live in.
- You are blessed to your bones and highly favored.
- Everyone and everything connected to you is blessed.
- Your children are blessed.
- Your business, career and ministry are blessed.
- You are blessed in your home and blessed when outside.
- The blessings of the Lord will follow you to all places.
- Grace and mercy follow you and favor will introduce you.
- Everyone will see the glory of God and the signature of God upon you; they will salute you and help you to greatness.
- Helpers of destinies will travel extra miles for your life; they will not rest until they help you to your reigning and shining.
- None will do you evil, all will favor and promote you.
- Refreshers of souls will surround you with the

resources to make your life colorful and fruitful.

- Oppression will be far away from you
- Affliction will be far away from you
- Poverty will be far away from you.
- Sickness will be far away from you; none will say, "I am sick' in your family.
- There will be no gathering of sorrow in your family.
- None will be found missing or wanting in your family.
- Whoever tries to hurt you will be hurt by warring angelic hosts.
- Evil eyes, evil hands, evil people trying to do you evil will experience closed heavens. They will grope in thick darkness day and night.
- Any enemy who rises against you will be defeated before you; they will fall, never to rise again.
- The mark of distinction of God rests upon your life; you are exempted from evil, calamity, drought, and premature death.
- You are the redeemed of the Lord; every time you return to your house, you will return with joyful shouting. Everlasting joy will be your portion; sorrow and shame will be far removed from you.
- Your heavens are permanently opened, in Jesus' name.

ABOUT THE AUTHOR

Dr. Anthonia Adeyeye, a.k.a Fire Prophetess, is a Microbiologist, Virologist, Educator, and a Life Coach. She is the senior Pastor of Abundant Life Christian Center, a ministry she co-founded and co-pastors with her husband, Dr. Festus Adeyeye.

She is a lover of God and enjoys God's presence hours on end. God recently gave her three different mantles (Miracles, Word, and Revelation) to foster her Prophetic Ministry and to raise end time harvests for God's kingdom.

As an ardent prayer warrior and an intercessor, she founded WWWW (Winning Women Weekend Warriors) – a dynamic impartation prayer forum that holds every Saturday evening for ladies within and outside the ALCC community. She also founded Morning Glory, a biweekly, insightful, powerful prayer teaching platform, exclusively for female Pastors and leading ladies in ministries.

As an energetic leader, Dr. Anthonia is the leading lady for the different departments for all women in ALCC,

Winners House – Winning Ladies, Golden Ladies, and Rubies & Diamonds. She is a witty leader, people lover, and very passionate about children, Dr. Anthonia is loved and adored by the ALCC family.

She is happily married to her childhood sweetheart, Dr. Festus Adeyeye, and she is passionately devoted to her amiable, tight-knit children and amazing grandchildren.

www.ingramcontent.com/pod-product-compliance
Lightning Source LLC
LaVergne TN
LVHW051834080426
835512LV00018B/2871